GOD
WHISPERS IN THE NIGHT

Marie Shropshire

HARVEST HOUSE PUBLISHERS
Eugene, Oregon 97402

D0583217

GOD WHISPERS IN THE NIGHT

Copyright © 1994 by Marie Shropshire
Published by Harvest House Publishers
Eugene, Oregon 97402

Library of Congress Cataloging-in-Publication Data

Shropshire, Marie, 1921–
        God whispers in the night / Marie Shropshire.
            p.   cm.
        ISBN 1-56507-285-5
        1. Christian life.   2. Shropshire, Marie, 1921– .   I. Title.
        BV4501.2.S447   1994   94-27674
        248.4—dc20   CIP

Printed in the United States of America.

    95   96   97   98   99   00   —   10   9   8   7   6   5   4   3

I dedicate this book
to the One who is always with me
even when I am not aware of His presence.
He whispers loving words to me
not only during my times of meditation
but any time I am open to His quiet voice.
He is always speaking to me—and to you.
He only asks that we tune in to Him
and listen for His gentle whispers.
He especially delights in whispering His love to us
in our nights of questions and struggles.
I pray that you will know experientially that
God whispers in the night.

Acknowledgments

First, I want to thank my friends, hundreds of whom I've never met, who were so enthusiastic about my book, *In Touch with God*, that they encouraged me to write another book.

Thanks go to several friends who came to me for prayer and shared with me their painful experiences. (Their names and the details of their stories have been changed.) Without them, Part Two of this book could not have been written.

I especially appreciate a particular loved one who so patiently taught me how to use a computer for writing this manuscript. In her humility, she asked me not to mention her name.

Thanks to Eileen Mason, LaRae Weikert, Bob Hawkins, and the other people at Harvest House Publishers who believed in *God Whispers in the Night* and felt the time had come to make it available to those who are listening for God's whispers in their nights of questioning.

Most importantly, I thank our heavenly Father for inspiring me and enabling me to write this book. I also thank Him for making me willing to become vulnerable. To be vulnerable is uncomfortable, almost frightening, but I want you to be able to identify with me and be blessed as I have been.

Preface

Part One of this book reflects my encounters with challenges along my spiritual path, followed by God's loving answers. Although it may seem a little threatening, I invite you to join me in my meditation times. I believe you will have some of the same questions I had, and that you will find the unfailing comfort and assurance I found.

Part Two deals with questions from some of my friends and God's loving answers to them. All names and details have been changed. If you think you recognize yourself or someone you know, it is only because the problems are universal.

I have discovered that God is not only holy and awesome but also a personal God, a loving, understanding Father who wants us to know Him intimately. His faithfulness is unchanging. He loves us as much as He loved Abraham, Isaac, Jacob, and all the other people of Bible days. He still speaks, not audibly but in our thoughts. He only asks that we declare with the psalmist, "I will listen to what God the Lord will say" (Psalm 85:8).

—Marie Shropshire

Contents

Preface

Part Two: He Answers My Friends

PART ONE

❧

He Answers Me

❧ 1 ❧

Unstable Emotions

ord, I'm disappointed in my-self. I don't like what's happening inside me. I'm up and then down. When I listen to an uplifting Bible teaching or I'm blessed by a Scripture passage during my quiet time, I feel fine for a while. I think, "I'm on my way to wholeness."

I'm reminded of who I am in you and life seems wonderful for several days, maybe even for a few weeks. I dare to hope I'll feel that way the rest of my life. Then one day I suddenly realize that my wonderful confident feeling has disappeared like the morning dew, and I'm down again. The pattern keeps repeating itself. A Christian ought not to be like this. What can I do about it?

*D*ear child, you are putting unnecessary *oughts* on yourself. Who says a Christian shouldn't be like this? Allow yourself to be human. You're still living in a fallen world, you know. You still live in a human body and are subject to its limitations.

Instead of being down on yourself when you feel less than your real self, encourage yourself with the thought that just as painful circumstances never last, neither do such feelings. They're always temporary. Life has its hurts and its interruptions, but it always picks up again. And you are wiser and stronger for your experiences.

You are growing and changing constantly. You're not the same as you were yesterday, last week, last year, or ten years ago. It happens so gradually that you're not aware of it. But growth is not necessarily steadily forward. That's all right. I accept you as you are.

Since you know your feelings are changeable, don't pay too much attention to them. Instead of trusting in your feelings, put your anchor in me. I never change. I am always dependable. My purposes are eternal, unchanging, perfect.

> The plans of the Lord stand firm forever,
> the purposes of his heart through all generations (Psalm 33:11).

When you're feeling down, you have difficulty being aware of my presence. The enemy would like to use that to keep you from communing with me. Don't let his suggestions affect your devotional life. I am as near you when you feel I'm a million miles away as when you're rejoicing in my presence. I never leave you.

Precious child, do you realize it's when you drive yourself hardest that you're most prone to gloomy feelings? Give yourself a break. Allow yourself to do some things just for fun. Stop taking yourself so seriously. The earth won't stop turning if you fail to get everything done in a day.

Even Jesus didn't work all the time. He took time to go fishing with His disciples. He called them aside to rest. He relaxed in the home of Mary and Martha. He enjoyed a wedding party.

Stop feeling guilty for your feelings. Remember that no one escapes occasional times of low spirits. Look at your shadowy times as opportunities for greater trust in me.

Refuse to struggle over anything you have no control over.

When your commitments become too much for you, give yourself permission to say no. The world won't fall apart.

Remind yourself that I'm in charge.

Rest in the knowledge that I am with you. Nothing can happen without my consent. You are my responsibility.

Join the psalmist in declaring, "You, O Lord, are a compassionate and gracious God, slow to anger, abounding in love and faithfulness" (Psalm 86:15). Bear that in mind next time you're tempted to give in to gloom. Your feelings are okay, but don't let them order you around.

Remember that you can't always be sure of your feelings, but you *can* always be sure of my love and faithfulness. That's what matters most.

❧ 2 ❧

Self-Doubt

ord, *in spite of all you've brought me through, I sometimes have feelings of self-doubt. My friends tell me such feelings are unfounded and that I shouldn't have them. But I find myself looking to other people for answers. Yet I know, at least with my intellect, that you have the answer to every question and that you speak to me as well as to others. Why am I like this? How can I change?*

*D**ear child*, some of the patterns of your past are still clinging to you. The circumstances of your life cause you to feel as if you're incapable of hearing me for yourself. That stems from your feelings of unworthiness and the lack of affirmation you have received. Your subconscious mind tells you that certain other people are more special and more worthy in my sight than you.

But I say to you that you are special in my heart simply because you belong to me. You are my workmanship, my poem, unique and valuable. I created you to be who you are—in spirit, in soul, and in body. I knitted you together in your mother's womb. You are fearfully and wonderfully made. Before you were born I scheduled every day of your life (Psalm 139:13-16). I set you apart for myself to be a part of my glorious inheritance.

Think of how my loving eyes see you. Regardless of how you see yourself, remember that you are special to me. Your specialness depends not on what others say, not on what others think, not on anything you do or fail to do, but on your relationship with me.

"I have summoned you by name; you are mine" (Isaiah 43:1). You belong to me; I am your loving Father. I have given you value. I take great delight in you. I rejoice over you with singing.

Your adversary often tries to trap you and make you feel unworthy of hearing from me. I have given you power over the enemy. Resist him and his accusations. As I rejoice over you, I want you to rejoice in me. I will keep you as the apple of my eye (Psalm 17:8).

Refuse thoughts of any negative thing anyone in your past has done or said. You have studied my Word. You have it in your heart. Trust my Spirit dwelling within you. My Word and my Spirit are always in agreement. You can put away self-doubt and trust me to give you answers based on my Word.

❧ 3 ❧

Troublesome Thoughts

Lord, sometimes my mind is bombarded with uninvited thoughts of things that happened in my past—regretful things I did or said, or things other people did or said to me. Your Word says, "Be transformed by the renewing of your mind" (Romans 12:2). When I'm having such thoughts, my mind is far from being renewed.

Neither am I allowing one of my favorite prayers to be fulfilled in me: "May the words of my mouth and the meditation of my heart be pleasing in your sight, O Lord, my Rock and my Redeemer" (Psalm 19:14). I want my life and my thoughts to be governed by your Word and your will, but if my thoughts are forever going astray, how can I do that?

I feel guilty for having thoughts that have nothing to do with where I am now. How can I keep thoughts that do not promote spiritual growth from coming or from lingering with me?

*P*recious child, you know that everything that ever happened to you is stored in your subconscious mind. You've been healed of the hurts caused by those happenings. But the happenings themselves cannot be deleted like unwanted words on your computer. You cannot keep these thoughts from coming to your mind any more than you can keep a salesman from knocking at your door.

But just as you do not have to invite the salesman into your house, neither do you have to invite the thoughts to linger in your mind. Do you feel guilty because the salesman appeared at your door? Of course not. Likewise, you have no reason to feel guilty for the thoughts that appear at the door of your mind. They come. Let them go.

Of course, they'll return unless you fill your mind and keep it filled with other thoughts. The apostle Paul suggested a way to handle that: "Since, then, you have been raised with Christ, set your hearts on things above, where Christ is seated at the right hand of God. Set your minds on things above, not on earthly things. For you died, and your life is now hidden with Christ in God" (Colossians 3:1-3).

Setting your mind on things above includes looking at yourself in terms of the exalted Christ and seeing yourself as indwelt by Him. As soon as you're aware of an unwanted thought, turn your thoughts immediately toward me. Quote Scriptures, sing a hymn, or turn on your tape player and listen to choruses or a tape of my Word or to an uplifting sermon or Bible teaching. Do that every time uninvited thoughts come, and soon you'll break their power over you.

You have read this statement by Oswald Chambers: "We must choose our thinking, and the whole discipline of our mental life is to form the habit of right thinking. It is not done by praying, it is done only by strenuous determination, and it is never easy to begin with."*

Because of the fallen world in which you live, controlling your thoughts is a challenge. But I live within you to assist you in accomplishing your task. With my help you can do it. Follow the suggestions I've given you. Remember that I am with you—never to condemn but to encourage.

---

* Kathleen M. Chambers, *Oswald Chambers* (Nashville: Oliver Nelson, 1987), pp. 357-58.

4

Discouragement

ord, sometimes I feel deep discouragement. I don't like to admit it, but I get discouraged about a lot of things that go on in my life and in the lives of others. Is that normal for a mature Christian? Or is

*it evidence of my lack of faith? How
can I deal with discouragement when
it strikes?*

Precious child, if you could see what I see,
you would know that every child of mine
experiences times of discouragement. Look into the
Scriptures and observe a few men who became discouraged. Consider Moses, Job, Elijah, David, Jonah,
and Jeremiah. You think of them as mature men of
faith, don't you?

Besides these and many more men and women of
Bible times, some of the best-known present-day
ministers of my gospel struggle with discouragement. It has been so ever since the fall in Eden. But
as you have read in Charles Swindoll's writings, no
pit is so deep that I am not deeper still, and no valley
so dark that the light of my truth cannot penetrate.

I realize that when you're discouraged, you may
feel as if you're having to drive through muddy ruts
created by someone else, or to walk through ankle-
deep puddles with no other path to follow.

Occasionally you feel so discouraged that your
body aches, and your emotions scream in the midst
of your frustration. But I always stand with hope for
my discouraged children: "The eyes of the Lord are
on those who fear him, on those whose hope is in his
unfailing love" (Psalm 33:18).

In your down times, rekindle the spark of hope that lies deep within you. The flame flickers low when deep disappointment strikes you. You may think the fire of hope has died, but you can fan the flame to life again. Hope always in me, in my Word, and in my ability to bring good from seeming evil. Put on hope as a helmet—covering your mind, guarding your thoughts. Wait quietly, patiently. You will not be disappointed. I am the God of hope. I will fill you with joy and peace.

Try losing yourself in an inspirational book. Good books can feed your soul when nothing else can. I not only speak to my children through my holy Word, but also in another sense through the writings of others.

Do not allow despair to destroy your hopes or to distract you from me. Declare with the psalmist, "We wait in hope for the Lord; he is our help and our shield" (Psalm 33:20).

The book of Psalms is a praise book. Use it often when you feel down. The time when you feel least like praising is the most needful time for you to praise. Praise long enough and your spirit will be lifted. The psalmists knew that and looked to me when everything seemed to be against them. They cried to me in despair, expressing their feelings of hopelessness. They didn't cry out in unbelief but in the light of hope.

The psalmists knew the truth of what J.B. Phillips expressed when he said we have "a God-shaped hole that only he can fill." Worshiping and praising when you feel the least like praising gives meaning to your life that nothing else can give. When you praise me, you turn your focus from yourself to me.

Acknowledging my presence, my love, and my power enables you to trust *me*, not the darkness, to control your thoughts and your life. Praising me for who I am and for my greatness helps to clarify your vision of who I really am.

Choose some of the prayers of the psalmists and pray them as your own. You might start with these:

> In you, O Lord, I have taken refuge; let me never be put to shame; deliver me in your righteousness. Turn your ear to me, come quickly to my rescue; be my rock of refuge, a strong fortress to save me.... Be strong and take heart, all you who hope in the Lord (Psalm 31:1,2,24).

> You make me glad by your deeds, O Lord; I sing for joy at the works of your hands. How great are your works, O Lord, how profound your thoughts! (Psalm 92:4,5).

> The Lord will not reject his people; he will never forsake his inheritance.... When I said, "My foot is slipping," your love, O Lord, supported me. When anxiety was great within me, your consolation brought joy to my soul.... The Lord has become my fortress, and my God the rock in whom I take refuge (Psalm 94:14,18,19,22).

All I was to David and the other psalmists I will be to you too. Put your hope and expectations in me alone and you will never be disappointed. You cannot always be sure of your moods, but you can always be sure of my love and faithfulness. That's what counts.

❧ 5 ❧

Feelings of Unworthiness

ℒord, I realize you've done a lot for me and through me, but I'm still plagued by feelings of unworthiness. When someone compliments my work or expresses appreciation for what I've done, I have difficulty

*accepting the compliments. There
lurks within me the old feeling that I
don't deserve to be recognized. What
do you have to say about this?*

*D***ear child**, it can be emotionally healthy to accept sincere praise. In your childhood and many times throughout your adult life, you heard a great deal about the need for humility. Humility is indeed commendable. But the teaching you heard was distorted.

To possess humility doesn't mean you are to degrade or devalue yourself, but to be modest and unpretentious. It means to recognize that your worth comes not from anything you do, but from me.

I created you in my image to have joyful fellowship with me. If you come cringing before me, our fellowship is anything but joyful. I invite you to come with the full assurance of acceptance, knowing that my Son's work on the cross was complete.

I died for you as if you were the only person on earth. You have received the gift of righteousness through Christ. You are worthy through Him. You are a new creation. You are filling a unique place in my kingdom. I created you, and then recreated you to be my friend, to have a love relationship with me, to enjoy fellowship with me. Everything you do matters to me.

You have heard one of my servants say repeatedly that you are a unique expression of my creative genius. You yourself have told others that. Accept the truth for yourself. Commune with me daily, hourly, moment by moment, and listen while I tell you how much I love you, how valuable you are to me, child of my heart. Revel in it. Never doubt it.

You are the salt of the earth (Matthew 5:13).

You are the light of the world (Matthew 5:14).

You are a temple of God. My Spirit dwells in you (1 Corinthians 3:16).

You are an expression of the life of Christ because He is your life (Colossians 3:4).

You are chosen of me, holy and dearly beloved (Colossians 3:12).

You are one of my living stones, being built up in Christ as a spiritual house (1 Peter 2:5).

"The Lord your God is with you, he is mighty to save. He will take great delight in you, he will quiet you with his love, he will rejoice over you with singing" (Zephaniah 3:17).

You are mine. You will never be able to discover all the benefits that belong to you simply because you are mine. The ocean cannot contain the love I have for you. I love you simply because you are you. I'm the one who knows you best and loves you most. I look at you through Christ's robe of righteousness.

Put away your doubts and rest in my love.

❧ 6 ❧

Feelings of Defeat

ord, I know you're in charge of my life, but sometimes I feel the trials you allow are almost too much for me. At those times I feel helpless and alone, defeated. What word do you have for me?

*D*ear child of mine, I understand how you feel. Would it make you feel better to know that your feelings and reactions are normal? Everyone experiences times when their trials seem unending and they feel crushed by defeat.

Trials are never intended to crush or weigh you down, causing you to feel cut off from me. But trials are a necessary part of your spiritual growth. Your struggles are meant to expose you to more of my love and grace. Would you not be inclined to depend on your own strength if you never faced problems beyond your human ability to handle?

When your life is invaded with trouble, remember that I have not abandoned you. It is the work of the enemy to make you feel alone. He would have you doubt my presence. But would I, your Creator, your Savior, leave you during a time of distress? "Never will I leave you; never will I forsake you" (Hebrews 13:5). "There is a friend who sticks closer than a brother" (Proverbs 18:24). I am that Friend.

Because of your trials, I can produce in you qualities which otherwise could not be. "You are precious and honored in my sight, and . . . I love you" (Isaiah 43:4). You are being fitted for further service in my kingdom. I am intimately involved in your life and in all that happens to you. I am *for* you, never against you.

Look past your circumstances to me. You are valuable to me. I have set you apart for myself. You are a member of a chosen people, a special people, holy in my sight, a people belonging to me, that you may declare my praise (1 Peter 2:9).

I have called you out of darkness into my wonderful light (1 Peter 2:9). When you're going through trials, you often feel as if you're *in the midst of darkness*, not delivered from it. Your feelings are not always trustworthy. Rely not on your feelings but on me and on my promises.

Look beyond feelings to reality. One day your feelings will catch up with truth. You will know that through every trial I am preparing you for something special. You will joyfully praise me. You will know that victory is yours.

7

Loneliness

Lord, only you and I know the heartache I experienced during that painful period several years ago. I never dreamed such things would ever happen to me. But true to your promise, you comforted me.

Constantly I found consolation in your Word, especially such passages as this one in Isaiah:

> *Fear not, for I have redeemed you;*
> *I have summoned you by name; you are mine.*
> *When you pass through the waters,*
> *I will be with you;*
> *and when you pass through the rivers,*
> *they will not sweep over you.*
> *When you walk through the fire,*
> *you will not be burned;*
> *the flames will not set you ablaze (Isaiah 43:1,2).*

You assured me that even though the circumstances which came to me were not in your perfect will, you would work out the experience for my good and your glory. Indeed, you have.

I could not have grown in my intimate knowledge of you and your personal love for me in any other way.

Neither could you have used me to be a blessing to thousands of hurting women as you have done. So I thank you, not only for the experience but for the pain it brought me.

Most of the time I feel fulfilled and blessed. But Lord, I cannot deny that I occasionally feel lonely. I long for someone with whom I can share daily experiences. What word do you have for me at such times?

*B*eloved child, I am aware of the loneliness you sometimes feel. I know and I care. In your times of loneliness you are sometimes tempted to feel neglected, forgotten, and forsaken. Others may neglect you, forget you, or forsake you, but I never will.

> Can a mother forget
>   the baby at her breast
>   and have no compassion
>   on the child she has borne?

Though she may forget,
    I will not forget you! (Isaiah 49:15).

In your daily quiet times, meditate on what I'm about to tell you.

Know that I long to fill the emptiness in your heart,
    to comfort you,
    to show you my compassion,
    to draw you to myself.

You are always welcome in my presence. I am waiting with open arms to pour out my love upon you.

Others may overlook you. Friends may forget you. Some may even betray you. In my walk on earth I experienced all of this. I know how it feels to be alone.

I am with you
    now
    and always.

I am as close to you as the air you breathe, as close as your own heartbeat. "Never will I leave you; never will I forsake you" (Hebrews 13:5).

You are mine.

You are precious to me.

You always will be.

As a good mother holds her hurting child close to her bosom, so I hold you close to my heart.

"As a mother comforts her child, so will I comfort you" (Isaiah 66:13).

I am with you when you feel like an orphan alone in the cold. I am with you in the heat of trials.

I will guide you and console you.

Remember that I am always present to assure you of my love. I am your very own personal comforter,

> your burden-bearer,
> the healer of your hurts.

I will bestow on you—

> a crown of beauty
> instead of ashes,
> the oil of gladness
> instead of mourning,
> and a garment of praise
> instead of a spirit of despair (Isaiah 61:3).

I am your indwelling Comforter.

Be especially aware

> of my indwelling presence
> of your union with me.

Your loneliness can create channels for you to know

> union with me,
> the joy of my indwelling presence.

Nothing can compare with the joy of knowing union with me. You are fulfilled in me.

Rest in the assurance that I am present

> ever
> and always.

❧ 8 ❧

Anxious Feelings

ord, with all that's going on in our country—rising crime rates, unjust laws, and so many uncertainties, I don't feel as safe as I used to. How can any of us be at peace within? So many things are changing, and it seems they're all for the worse. How can I keep from living without a sense of anxiety and uneasiness?

*B*eloved child of mine, I understand your fears regarding these sensitive, anxiety-inducing times. You are feeling the way so many people of the world are feeling at this time. Remember that you belong to me and I watch over my own. Now is a good time to focus especially on me. Lean your entire being on me and receive my love.

Many things are changing indeed. But I never change. I am always faithful to my promises to my children. I have promised to care for you, regardless of circumstances.

Look into Scripture and see how situations were constantly challenging during Bible times. My people were often threatened in various ways. They didn't know what to do. Did I ever fail any of those who trusted in me? My servant David is a good example. Do you remember how he had to flee for his life when King Saul determined to put an end to his existence? But my hand was upon him to protect him.

Later David wrote:

I will sing of the Lord's great love forever;
with my mouth I will make your faithfulness known through all generations....

O Lord God Almighty, who is like you?
You are mighty, O Lord, and your faithfulness surrounds you (Psalm 89:1,8).

Your fearful circumstances will not exactly dup-
licate David's, but you must know, precious child,
that dreadful times are bound to come. My Word
warns of that. You can affirm, even before such
times come, the same truth that David did. You can
avow as David did at another time:

My eyes are fixed on you, O Sovereign
Lord; in you I take refuge (Psalm 141:8).

As you fix your eyes on me, remember to put into
practice what Paul wrote to young Timothy:

I urge, then, first of all, that requests,
prayers, intercession and thanksgiving
be made for everyone—for kings and all
those in authority, that we may live peaceful and quiet lives in all godliness and
holiness (1 Timothy 2:1,2).

Quiet and peaceful living is always my desire for
my people. Even when it seems that everything in
your world is going wrong, you can still have inner
peace because of your knowledge of me. How accu-
rately the psalmist said of me:

> The Lord is gracious and compassionate,
> slow to anger and rich in love. The Lord is
> good to all; he has compassion on all he
> has made (Psalm 145:8,9).

In the midst of seeming darkness, remember that you and your generation of Christians are as much my chosen people as the Israelites of old. You belong to me just as they did. I care for you just as I did for them. You are always under the umbrella of my protection.

> He who dwells in the shelter of the Most
> High will rest in the shadow of the Al-
> mighty.... "Because he loves me," says
> the Lord, "I will rescue him; I will protect
> him, for he acknowledges my name"
> (Psalm 91:1,14).

I never break any of my promises. Remember this one:

> When the enemy shall come in like a
> flood, the Spirit of the Lord shall lift up a
> standard against him (Isaiah 59:19 KJV).

You have seen how the spiritual enemy has come in, working such evil as prohibiting prayer and Bible reading in many public places. That has frightened you. I will lift up my standard against him. You will see my promise fulfilled. Have no fear.

As your worship and fellowship with me become more constant, you will be less fearful. You will be more at peace, more aware of my loving care. I am not fretting over world conditions; I know the outcome. Neither are you to fret, but to trust me. You can pray and be concerned and intercede without losing your peace. Peace is my gift to you. Receive it with joy. Rest in it.

❧ 9 ❧

Distractions

ord, *too often during my early-morning times of private worship, my mind wanders to other subjects. Sometimes I start making plans for the day. At other times, instead of letting you speak to my*

*heart, I may start thinking about
how I can use the Scriptures I've just
read to help someone else. I'm sure
you've noticed this and it must
offend you. It certainly displeases
me. What can I do?*

*D*ear child, you made the first step toward correcting your problem when you recognized what you were doing. But let me assure you it's bothering you a lot more than it's bothering me.

Don't get overly upset with yourself for allowing yourself to become distracted. Allow yourself to be human. I know your desire is to please me. That's what matters most to me. I always look first at heart motives.

Now let's get to some reasons you're being distracted while worshiping. Do you recall when you were packing to move to your present location how much clutter you had to get rid of? You found after living in your other house so many years you had accumulated a lot of things you didn't need—things that would be in your way after you moved. You discovered there is "a time to keep and a time to throw away" (Ecclesiastes 3:6).

Your spiritual life is like that too. Even as you found things on your shelves and in your closets which reduced your effectiveness and kept you from being orderly and organized, so you have a few things buried in your mind that hinder your spiritual effectiveness. For example, much of your past teaching and your culture have taught you to be always outwardly busy. Too little emphasis has been placed on the need for inner quiet.

You feel that you need to *do* certain things in order to please me. Let go of that idea and realize I want your life to be a celebration of who you are in me. Let everything be done joyously and unhurriedly, simply remembering that I live within you to work through you. Let go of the pressure. I don't want you to be so busy with the mundane things of life that you're unable to quiet your mind and focus on me and enjoy my love.

Get rid of the ideas that limit your understanding of my personal love. Live in such awareness of my loving presence that you know I will be with you in all your work, regardless of its nature. Never doubt my care of you. I rejoice in our fellowship. My greatest desire is to bless you.

As for your mind turning to how you can use the Scriptures to help others, you know, without my reminding you, that any blessing you give to others must come from the overflow of your own heart. You need not condemn yourself for this kind of mind-wandering. It's natural for you to think of others while you're reading my Word. When you do, stop and pray for them and then return to your Bible reading.

If you will enjoy me and my peace and stop striving and fretting about your mind wandering, you'll find it wanders less. Think of Paul's words, "It is God who works in you to will and to act according to his good purpose" (Philippians 2:13). Trust me to take care of the work within you. Refuse to be frustrated by your distractions. You are on a path of growth.

❧ 10 ❧

More Joy Needed

ord, I need more of your joy in my life. I grew up taking life too seriously. For example, when I was a very young child I always dreaded summer revival time. Everyone cried. I don't remember ever seeing anyone express joy in church.

I concluded that Christianity must be serious and solemn. I'm glad that in spite of those feelings, I accepted your salvation at an early age. But I'm sorry I missed the joy which I now see as part of your plan. I think those early influences still affect my life.

Maybe I'm not the only one who feels the negative impact of past religious experiences. I read recently that joy is the most needed ingredient in contemporary Christianity. The writer said the secret of Jesus was His inner joy. Then why is He referred to as a man of sorrows? And why do we not see more joy in our churches? How can I change my past mental programming?

*C*hild of mine, you're right. You're not the only one who has missed much of the joy I intended for my followers. Joylessness in Christianity was true of many in the generation preceding yours and has carried over into numerous churches of today. Some of my people equate spirituality with being somber. They haven't seen the truth expressed by my apostle Paul when he said:

> The kingdom of God is not a matter of eating and drinking, but of righteousness, peace and joy in the Holy Spirit (Romans 14:17).

My Son became a man of sorrows when He bore the sins of the world on the cross. But He *joyfully* gave His life. "[Jesus] for the joy set before him endured the cross" (Hebrews 12:2). He looked ahead to the joy of heaven and to the joy He would bring to others through His death and resurrection.

My Son was joyful because He knew who He was and why He came. Would crowds have flocked to Him if He had not been a man of joy? Would His twelve apostles have sought His presence continually if He had exuded sorrow? Would mothers have brought their little children to Him for blessing if He had not been a man who radiated joy?

My people have failed to grasp the truth spoken by my prophet Isaiah when he said my Son came in order to—

> provide for those who grieve in Zion—to bestow on them a crown of beauty instead of ashes, the oil of gladness instead of mourning, and a garment of praise instead of a spirit of despair (Isaiah 61:3).

Look around at the beautiful world I created for my pleasure and yours. It's an expression of my joy. My desire is for you to "be glad and rejoice forever in what I [have created], for I [have created it all] to be a delight and [my] people a joy" (Isaiah 65:18).

My apostle Peter wrote that those who believed in me in his time were "filled with an inexpressible and glorious joy" (1 Peter 1:8). That's exactly what I want for you. I am your source of joy.

My written Word is filled with references to joy, but you have missed many of them. Rejoice, dear child, as you consider these words:

> Shout for joy to the Lord, all the earth, burst into jubilant song with music; make music to the Lord with the harp, with the harp and the sound of singing, with trumpets and the blast of the ram's horn—shout for joy before the Lord, the King (Psalm 98:4-6).

Doesn't that sound as if I want you to be joyful? And look at Isaiah's words bubbling with effervescence:

> You will go out in joy and be led forth in peace; the mountains and hills will burst into song before you, and all the trees of the field will clap their hands (Isaiah 55:12).

Take a new look at my Son's Sermon on the Mount. It's a picture of who you are—a child to be blessed, happy. The beatitudes begin with "Blessed are..." The word *blessed* means to be gloriously happy in spite of circumstances.

My desire is for you to be so happy that your heart dances with joy. Your celebration of joy is to include both private and public worship, just as it did for my people in Bible times.

> Rejoice in the Lord always. I will say it again: Rejoice! (Philippians 4:4).

> Shout for joy to the Lord, all the earth. Worship the Lord with gladness; come before him with joyful songs (Psalm 100:1,2).

Your joy is never to depend upon circumstances but in knowing I'm in charge. When my early disciples were persecuted for preaching the good news of my salvation, they "were filled with joy and with the Holy Spirit" (Acts 13:52). They knew they were in my will and that I was in charge of whatever happened.

As you read your Bible look for examples of joy. You'll be surprised at how often you'll find them. Meditate on those passages. Soak in them. Make them yours.

Find something every day to laugh about. Remember the story of Charles Spurgeon? One day when he and a group of his preacher friends were criticized for laughing instead of being somber, he continued laughing. Then he praised me, saying, "Thank you, God, for laughter. I know you're laughing with us."

The message of salvation is one of joy and gladness. "I have come that they may have life, and have it to the full" (John 10:10). So accept my joy, dear one. It's yours. Live in it. "I have told you this so that my joy may be in you and that your joy may be complete" (John 15:11).

· 11 ·

Insecurity

*Lord, I don't know whether it's
my failure to trust you sufficiently or for some other reason,
but sometimes I feel terribly insecure.
With my intellect I know you're
faithful to your promises to supply*

*all my needs. But my heart needs to
get the message. What can I do about
these unwanted feelings?*

Child of mine, I am aware of your feelings of insecurity. I understand, and I want you to stop feeling guilty about how you feel. Your feelings are being affected by the circumstances of your childhood, when your family had to be so careful about every penny they spent.

Your obsession with your needs causes you to doubt my provision. Too often you have asked yourself, "What if . . . ? Can I be sure of . . . ?" As you relive the past you see false "reasons" to doubt whether I will provide.

Dear child, think about this: Have I failed you yet? Often I have allowed you to *wait* for your supply. I do that to develop your faith. My objective is to teach you to walk not by sight, as the world does, but by faith. You are mine. I never fail to provide for my own.

Meditate on this truth: I, the Creator of all things, am your Shepherd, a Shepherd who watches over His sheep, a Shepherd who knows and cares and supplies every need.

Remember, dear child, "The Lord is [your] shepherd, [you] shall not [be in] want" (Psalm 23:1). No good thing do I withhold from my sheep. My divine power has given you everything you need for life and godliness through your knowledge of me (Psalm 84:11; 2 Peter 1:3).

Meditate often on my Word. Focus on my promises. Become more deeply aware of my abiding presence, of my love, of my desire to bless you. I have charged myself with your care. I have redeemed your past. You need no longer live with a sense of fear, anxiety, or future peril.

When circumstances appear calamitous, remind yourself that I am your Shepherd and I am in control. I take delight in seeing you contented, resting in me, confident of my care.

As a human shepherd is concerned when his sheep are restless, so I look with concern upon you when you are agitated, when you are unaware of my love and care, of my provision. As Eastern shepherds led their flocks into lush green meadows and beside quiet waters, I invite you to walk with me in quiet confidence, in intimate fellowship with me.

I long for you to live in joy, peace, tranquility. I guide you into paths of righteousness for my name's sake. When I allow you to walk through the valley, I have a good reason for it. Remember that I have walked there. I know the path. I will hold your hand, and we will walk together. You need not fear. You will find refreshment in the midst of difficulties.

My blessings will flow to you through crevices chiseled out by misfortunes of the past. When the enemy assails you, my Word will sustain you, instruct you, encourage you, and give you peace.

Regardless of what comes your way, look to me, trust all to me. Refuse to allow circumstances to threaten your feelings of security. I will not fail you. Goodness and mercy will follow you always. You will dwell forever surrounded by my presence. I am with you. I am for you.

ᵃ 12 *ᵃ*

Needing Assurance
of God's Love

*Lord, in my heart I know you're
a God of love. But I don't feel
your love as I would like to. In my
childhood and much of my adult
life I heard little preaching and
teaching of your love. I'm sure that*

*my understanding of the depth of
your love is not all it should be. I need
a greater assurance of your unconditional love for me.*

*Too many preachers in my past
emphasized hellfire and damnation.
I learned to see you as a God so stern
and demanding that one would want
to accept your salvation in order to
escape hell and avoid your wrath, not
necessarily to accept your goodness
and love. What do you have to say to
me about this?*

*P*recious child, how well I understand. I long
for you to know the fullness of my love. You're
far from being the only one who lacks a true understanding of the depth of my love. Many reject me
because they have seen nothing of my unconditional
love.

Many who know me as Savior are wearing themselves out striving to please me because they believe
they have to earn my continued love. They fear I'll
bring disaster upon them unless they fulfill certain
rules and regulations. They live in dread of my
wrath. How far this is from my will!

I wish my people understood that my wrath is poured out only on those who deliberately refuse my love and rebel against me. Hell was prepared for the devil and his angels. "The reason the Son of God appeared was to destroy the devil's work" (1 John 3:8). Only those who hear my Word and willfully reject me will join the enemy in that dreadful place.

My holy love causes me to hate sin but love sinners. My love is boundless, unlimited. It reaches to all, because I *am* love. The cross of Calvary proves my unconditional love for you and for all of creation.

Hundreds of times you have read or quoted, "For God so loved the world that he gave his one and only Son, that whoever believes in him shall not perish but have eternal life" (John 3:16). But often you've overlooked the following verse: "For God did not send his Son into the world to condemn the world, but to save the world through him" (John 3:17).

I am not a condemning Father. I am all-loving, always ready to forgive. That's why my Son told the parable of the prodigal son. I wait with open arms for my wandering ones to return. I have chosen to bind myself to a covenant of love with you. I cannot fail you. When you understand that my love is better than life itself, you will declare with the psalmist, "Because your love is better than life, my lips will glorify you" (Psalm 63:3).

Remember your mother's favorite Scripture verse:

How great is the love the Father has lavished on us, that we should be called children of God! And that is what we are! (1 John 3:1).

Come to me and simply be aware of my love. Know that all your sins are blotted out. You need not always come confessing past sins. They were paid for on the cross. I forgave you the first time you asked. Relax and let me love you. I delight to show you my love.

You were included when my Son prayed:

May they be brought to complete unity to let the world know that you sent me and have loved them even as you have loved me (John 17:23).

I answered His prayer, of course. Can you grasp the incredible truth that I love you as much as I loved my Son? It's true. Meditate on it. Revel in it.

Know also that as you can do nothing to earn my love, neither can anything separate you from my love:

Who shall separate us from the love of Christ? Shall trouble or hardship or persecution or famine or nakedness or danger or sword?...No, in all these things we are more than conquerors through him who loved us. For I am convinced that neither death nor life, neither angels nor demons, neither the present nor the future, nor any powers, neither height nor depth, nor anything else in all creation, will be able to separate us from the love of God that is in Christ Jesus our Lord (Romans 8:35-39).

When you comprehend how much I love and cherish you, a new joy will flood your soul. Many of life's troubles and questions will no longer bother you.

You have in your intellect much that I have told you. But, precious child, head knowledge is never sufficient. Everyone needs desperately to *feel* loved. No person on earth can give you all the love you need. You must feel my love in order to feel secure in this world.

Security comes not from people or circumstances. It comes from knowing deep within that I love you. Jesus came to give you abundant life, but unless you feel loved, you will not live the abundant life he provided.

I created you to love you. My greatest delight is in loving you and having you love me in return. You have difficulty letting me love you because the world has taught you to be self-sufficient.

Dare to take time daily to let me love you. Be quiet from your schedule of doing for others and know that the most important thing you can do is to let me love you.

❧ 13 ❧

Questions
About Prayer

ℒord, I've prayed every day as far back as I can remember, yet sometimes I feel as if I still don't know how to pray. Maybe it's my lack of self-confidence, but every time I hear others' testimonies of how they pray, I think, "I need to be praying like that."

One man says he always hears you speak when he prays. Another says if we don't pray audibly, we aren't praying. Some people tell us to follow prayer formulas. Still others say we must pray a certain number of minutes every day.

I don't do any of those things consistently. I don't think I've ever followed a formula. Is something wrong with my prayer life? Should I hear you speak every time I pray?

*D**ear child of mine**,* relax. You can learn from others' experiences without imitating them. What works best for them might not work at all for you. Those who say that prayer must be done a certain way have found the way that works best for them. You need not feel intimidated by their suggestions.

Never fret about prayer forms. Above everything else, I want you to be aware of my love. Be aware of my presence and let me love you. That's prayer. Those who offer formulas are often speaking to

Christians who feel they don't know how to pray on their own. Prayer for most people needs to be spontaneous.

Prayer includes listening, to be sure. But as for hearing my voice, don't feel bad about not hearing me as often as you would like. My voice is exceedingly quiet. But never strain to hear me speak. I often speak in ways you're not aware of. I speak in your thoughts. I speak throughout your day, not simply during your quiet time.

Don't let anyone put you in bondage regarding the number of minutes to pray. A person whose love life with me is developed wants to spend time with me. Prayer is not an obligation to fulfill but an opportunity to enjoy fellowship with me. It is opening yourself to receive the gift of myself. I am a lover, not a taskmaster.

As for audible prayer, there is no more value in that than in silent prayer. Continue as you're doing, praying according to the way that seems most natural for you at any given moment. Realize that it is I who take the initiative. Your prayer is your response to me. Your inspiration to pray may come through reading the Scriptures or through your thoughts and feelings.

Do you not find when you're dissatisfied with your prayer life, it is at a time when you're not sufficiently aware of my loving presence? Or at a time when you're feeling unworthy? Remember that you are worthy through Christ. Reject false feelings of guilt.

Realize that your union with me does not depend on *your* love but upon mine. Cultivate a consciousness of your union with me. I'm always near, even within you. You cannot enjoy communing with me if you perceive me as a far-off, judgmental God.

I am always present. You don't have to do anything to earn my presence. Prayer is giving yourself to me. Forget what you've heard regarding rule-keeping. Prayer is to be enjoyed, not endured. Let your primary purpose in prayer be to worship me and enjoy my presence.

Never measure the success of your prayer life by anyone else's experience. You are growing into the person I created you to be. Accept yourself and your prayer life without trying to do what is unnatural for you. You will find your own methods of prayer changing from time to time and varying from day to day. That's natural.

"I am the Lord your God, who teaches you what is best for you, who directs you in the way you should go" (Isaiah 48:17). This includes your prayer life. Rest in that assurance.

• 14 •

Being or Doing?

Lord, all my life I've heard such admonitions as, "Keep busy," "Don't waste your time," and "Get more work accomplished." As you know, our culture emphasizes the value of always doing, doing, doing.

Productivity takes priority over every-thing.

The longer I live, the less I see this as aligning with your teaching. If I'm always doing, there's no time for be-ing—being alone with you and being alone with myself long enough to know who I am. What do you say?

*D*ear child, how right you are. Life must have balance. And remember, "However many years a man may live, let him enjoy them all" (Ecclesiastes 11:8). How can you enjoy your years if you're always busy, rushing from one project to another? Even a venture undertaken for me needs to be left to someone else if it robs you of time to *be*. I love you for who you *are*, not for what you *do*.

Doing affects behavior. It's an outside event. *Being* occurs inside. When you take care of *being* who you are, proper doing will take care of itself.

The Pharisees were doers. Don't be like them. Don't get so caught up in the frenzy of work, even *good* work, that you forget the meaning of life. Life is for enjoying me and my creation. You need time with me in order to be fulfilled.

Your spirit, soul, and body require periods of rest and rejuvenation. "It is vain for you to rise up early, to take rest late, to eat the bread of [anxious] toil; for he gives [blessings] to His beloved in sleep" (Psalm 127:2 AMP). A weary body prevents your receiving all the blessings I have for you.

I am a God of love and compassion. I never drive my children. I desire only the best for you, ever and always.

It is not your service I want. It's you. I do not measure your worth by your productivity. You are valuable to me simply because you are you. I created you not to work for me but to love you and to express myself through you. "I will maintain my love to [you] forever, and my covenant with [you] will never fail" (Psalm 89:28).

"For as high as the heavens are above the earth, so great is his love for those who fear him" (Psalm 103:11). Affirm that truth with David and rest in the assurance of my love, knowing that I want you to *be*, not *do*.

• 15 •

Time Pressure

ord, it seems that I should not feel the pressure of time as I do. I never have enough time to get everything done in a day that I want to. I enjoy life and all that I do, but too often I feel rushed. I seem to be

*so slow. I've never been as speedy as
some people, but at this stage of my
life I've really slowed down. I'm yours
and my time is yours. But if I'm so
slow, am I not failing to be a good
steward of my time?*

*D*ear child, aren't you examining yourself
too critically again and expecting too much
of yourself? I am satisfied with you just as you are.
Regardless of how rapidly or slowly you move and
however much you accomplish in a day or in a year, I
am pleased with you. You are still the beloved child
of my heart.

Consider that living alone naturally puts additional claims on your time. Also take into consideration that you're not as young as you once were. Shouldn't you expect the added years to slow you down? Of course that doesn't mean you're any less valuable. Age brings spiritual wisdom and maturity while it brings less rapidity of outward movement.

Time affects all that you are. Time involves your sharing with me, growing in me, and developing your spiritual gifts. Time is also my gift to you. When you share a large portion of your time in communion with me, realize that you're giving me a gift—a gift that brings delight to my heart.

You might feel less pressure if you took a little more time simply to think about such things as the beauty and variety of the seasons of the year. Remember that I create each season and each day for your enjoyment. Respond to each day—not thinking about all you need to cram into it, but quietly and unhurriedly thinking about what the day offers. I provide you with enough time for everything I want you to do.

> There is a time for everything, and a season for every activity under heaven (Ecclesiastes 3:1).

Dear child, are you sometimes living tomorrow before it comes? Or are you trying to relive yesterday? Are you trying to make up for "lost" time? Life is for living one day at a time. Planning ahead is fine, but don't fret about whether you'll get enough done today, or worry about whether tomorrow will afford sufficient time to achieve all you hope for. Never look back with regret at yesterday or be overly concerned about tomorrow. Live today.

Time is for enjoyment. Time is for growth in me and knowledge of me. It is for appreciating the gifts I give you. Time is for caring for yourself and others. Time is for self-acceptance. I accept you as you are. Learn to accept yourself and your limitations.

Achievement of goals is less important than you think. And accomplishment is of less significance than enjoying my love. Our time together is like the fragrance of a garden of roses. The time you give to *things* is like a field of dry grass in comparison.

Be content with what you can accomplish each day, knowing that it is pleasing to me. When you are preoccupied with how much you can accomplish, you miss some of the joy I have for you. Live one day at a time in the blessing of my smile of love upon you.

ꙮ 16 ꙮ

Disappointment
with People

*ord, I have many faithful
friends, and I thank you for
them. But there are some who dis-
appoint me. I probably shouldn't let it
bother me, but it disturbs me deeply
for anyone to make a promise and*

fail to keep it. Do I expect too much of some people?

*D*ear child, I can identify with your feelings. Throughout my Son's walk on earth He constantly met people who disappointed us. All people are weak and must be accepted as they are. Remember my dear disciple Peter? He always meant well. Yet his weaknesses sometimes kept him from fulfilling the promises he made.

Most people who make promises and then break them do not mean to do so. Their intentions are as good as Peter's. In many cases they simply have so many responsibilities that they simply never get around to doing everything they intend to do. Others are burdened with personal problems.

Now that I've explained that, may I remind you of an important fact? When your eyes are on me alone, you need not pay attention to what others do to you or fail to do for you. Why should anything of this world matter if you're lost in my love?

When you look at what others are doing or failing to do, you forget that I'm in charge. All people are my responsibility. Don't let their failures (or what you perceive as failures) be of concern to you. They are growing in their own way, just as you are doing. Everyone is on a different path, and I accept them according to where they are at any given moment.

When I look at my children, I see them not as they are now but as they will become. I have a special blueprint for each life. You can help in the growth process of others if you will learn to see them only as my beloved children. See them maturing in me as they grow in their knowledge of me and of my love.

Rejoice in my love and grace. Know that my eye is upon you to care for you. Don't concern yourself with the shortcomings of yourself or others. Talk to me about them and then let them go. Leave the results to me. Know that my plans will be fulfilled.

Remember that "he who began a good work in you [and in your friends and acquaintances] will carry it on to completion until the day of Christ Jesus" (Philippians 1:6).

· 17 ·

A Wasted Day

Lord, I hope never to repeat a day like today. Last night I slept little because of my neighbor's noisy all-night party. I allowed that to affect my mood today. Everything I did went wrong. I feel like the little boy who described his day as a "hor-rible, terrible, no-good, very bad day."

First, I made yeast bread and forgot to add salt. My bread rose and then fell flat, resulting in a loaf half the size it should have been. Next, I made stew. After placing it on the burner I came expectantly to my office to write. Nothing flowed. My words sounded stilted.

When mealtime came and I returned to the kitchen, I discovered I'd forgotten to lower the burner under my stew. The stew had burned and the kitchen was filled with smoke. Now my whole house smells like smoke. (I wonder why I didn't notice the odor sooner?)

My whole day was wasted. I accomplished nothing worthwhile. I even forgot that you were present with me.

My dear child, who says your day was wasted? You learned from it, didn't you? No learning experience is totally wasted.

Of course, allowing your neighbors to control your mood proved to be the most detrimental thing you could have done. You took your eyes off me and forgot to let me reprogram your mind. If you had lingered longer with me during your quiet time this morning, and dealt with your feelings concerning your neighbor, your day could have gone more productively.

But now you realize that. And there's no need to look back or feel guilty. So just cuddle up in my lap and let me love you and remind you that absolutely nothing can separate you from my love. Let the awareness of my love and acceptance bring comfort to your heart, release to your mind, and rest to your body.

Let go of your discouragement concerning today. Recall David's words and make them yours: "When I said, 'My foot is slipping,' your love, O Lord, supported me.... Your consolation brought joy to my soul" (Psalm 94:18,19).

As I comforted and encouraged David, so I will do for you. Regardless of how you feel, regardless of what may have come against you today, you can be confident in me. Tomorrow will be another day, a day of opportunity and blessing. Look toward it with joyful anticipation. Remember that I will be with you.

❧ 18 ❧

Dreading
the Future

*ord, after church service this
morning, a friend read something to a group of us, something that
more than disturbs me. It causes me
to dread what the future may hold.
It regards laws which an influential*

*group of people are pushing to pass
for our schools. They want to begin
in kindergarten, teaching innocent
little children things I didn't know (or
need to know) until after I married.*

*All day I've had difficulty keeping
my mind from being occupied with
the possible impending disaster in our
nation if these evil-inspired laws are
passed.*

*B*eloved child, your concern is also my concern. I placed this knowledge before you so you could intercede for everyone involved. However, I want you to pray in hope, not in despair.

In a sense, your nation is in a similar condition to the nation of Judah during the time of Habakkuk. During his time, many people disregarded my law. Chastisement for their gross sins was inevitable. Habakkuk bore a heavy burden concerning what might happen. But I assured him I would protect the righteous and that they would eventually triumph. Putting his trust in my faithfulness, Habakkuk made this declaration:

> Though the fig tree does not bud and
> there are no grapes on the vines, though

> the olive crop fails and the fields produce
> no food . . . yet I will rejoice in the Lord, I
> will be joyful in God my Savior. The Sov-
> ereign Lord is my strength; he makes my
> feet like the feet of a deer, he enables me
> to go on the heights (Habakkuk 3:17-19).

Notice that Habakkuk didn't say he would be *happy*. He said he would be *joyful in me.* Joyfulness and happiness can be completely different. Happiness often means having no problems. To be joyful is to have faith in me in spite of happenings.

Habakkuk could be joyful because he turned from his worry about circumstances to trust in me. That is exactly what I want you to do. Pray for the circumstances surrounding you, but meanwhile trust in me. Then you can say as Habakkuk did, "The Lord is my strength. I will be joyful in him."

You need not be swept into the undertow of stressful times. I will strengthen you. You don't have to lean on your own strength. Lean entirely on me.

Focus on my just judgments and my unfailing love. Let my peace flood your soul. Rest in me. Be joyful in me.

❧ 19 ❧

Ups and Downs

*L*ord, *I've been rereading Gab-rielle Bossis' book* He and I. *Most of the time I find it inspiring and helpful, pointing me to a more intimate relationship with you. But at other times it discourages me because*

*I don't measure up to her level of
spirituality. I have up and down
feelings.*

*I view Gabrielle as a saint always
deeply aware of your loving presence.
In contrast, I see myself as one who
feels your nearness for periods of
time, then for days go with no real
sense of your being near me. Of
course I know you are near, but I
don't like not being aware of you as I
go about my necessary duties in the
house.*

*P*recious child, do you realize what you're
doing? You're comparing yourself with others. I
remind you once more that I didn't create you to be a
carbon copy of anyone else.

You're not the only one who has been overly
concerned about her feelings. Remember Hannah
Whitall Smith, whose books have blessed you im-
measurably. Do you recall that she went through a
ten-year period of skepticism simply because she
didn't *feel* my presence?

Later she referred to that period of her life as a
time of morbid self-introspection. By broadening
her interests to include other things, she freed her

mind to take a different view of herself and religion. She then realized that feelings must never be depended on as a test for one's depth of spirituality.

When the enemy said to Martin Luther, "Do you feel you're a child of God?" Luther replied, "No, I do not feel it at all, but I know it. Get thee behind me, Satan."

Whether it's the enemy or your self-introspection that causes you to get down on yourself when you're unaware of my presence, dismiss it. Hannah Smith discovered that struggling with her feelings never made them what she thought they should be. Remember, as she had to learn, that facts are far more important than feelings.

Madame Jeanne Guyon, another devoted disciple whose books you treasure, experienced a long period when she never felt my presence. Yet she never doubted. She continued reading my Word and talking to me. She didn't hear me speak apart from my written Word. She simply relied on what she knew to be truth, and that was sufficient for her.

One thing you can do to encourage yourself during those times when you are unable to feel my presence is to set aside a few minutes twice a day just to remind yourself of my indwelling presence. It need not necessarily be a time of so-called prayer, but only a quiet relaxing time alone with me. Don't try to work up any feelings. Just know that I love you. Simply *realize* that I'm with you, loving you.

⋅ 20 ⋅

Pushing Myself

Lord, I find that often I push myself and try to accomplish more than I'm capable of doing in a given time. Even though I realize this is not of you, I don't know how to get rid of what causes me to be like this.

*P*recious child, one reason you have this problem is that you're a product of your culture. Your world continually says, "Be strong. Be independent. It's all up to you."

It is difficult for my children to remain unaffected by the Western world's notions. Many of my people have fallen into the trap of self-sufficiency and overwork.

Another reason for your self-pressure is your self-image. Deep within you is the sense that you must prove to yourself that you can do everything you want to do. If you were more secure in the knowledge that I treasure you just as you are, you would be less inclined to pressure yourself.

I'm glad you recognize it's not *I* pushing you. If you thought it were I, you would feel guilty about not achieving more. Take time daily to remind yourself that you need do only what is reasonable to do. Since I'm not asking you to be a superperson, why should you require it of yourself?

I'm not in a hurry. I am always patient. Follow my example of patience. Be more patient with yourself. You don't have to earn my love by doing anything. I see your life from beginning to end. It's all under my control.

A subtle feeling lurks within you that the economy of the world may affect you adversely. That feeling presses you to accomplish all you can. You *are not* and *will not* be a victim of the economy or of fate.

You are my responsibility. I am arranging every detail of every circumstance pertaining to your life. As I said to Joshua, so I say to you:

> No one will be able to stand up against you all the days of your life. As I was with Moses, so I will be with you; I will never leave you nor forsake you (Joshua 1:5).

With that awareness, will you let go of your pressure on yourself and relax in me? I created you not to be independent or self-sufficient, but to be dependent on me.

I, who have given you eternal life and prepared heaven for you, am the same God who delivers you daily from the world's anxieties. I am faithful to my promises. I never change. "For great is [my] love, higher than the heavens; [my] faithfulness reaches to the skies" (Psalm 108:4).

❧ 21 ❧

Heaviness

*Lord, I feel the burden of many
who are in need of prayer. I'm
glad to be an intercessor. I count it
a privilege to pray for friends and
loved ones and for our country. But
sometimes I feel the burden is too*

*much for me. It's affecting my
physical body. I feel worn out. What
shall I do?*

*B*eloved child, you have taken on more than I
intended for you. I want you to intercede as
you're doing, but without feeling the pressure. Pray,
believing I have heard, and then release the care to
me. Don't be weighted down with care and anxiety
that is mine alone to bear.

Continuing to feel burdened can tempt you to
stop praying for others. That's what the enemy desires. Remember the words of Paul:

> Do not be anxious about anything, but in
> everything, by prayer and petition, with
> thanksgiving, present your requests to
> God. And the peace of God, which tran-
> scends all understanding, will guard your
> hearts and your minds in Christ Jesus
> (Philippians 4:6,7).

When you present your requests with thanksgiving, as Paul says, you know that I have heard your
prayer. You may choose to pray until you feel the
assurance that I have heard your prayer. Then you
can leave the results to me and let my peace fill your
mind.

The peace I give is a peace the world cannot understand. When you were hurting so badly several years ago, you finally realized your prayer would not be answered in the way you had hoped. Yet you had peace, knowing that I would take care of you.

A burden doesn't have to weigh you down to the point that you want to fly away from life and its situations. When you pray, you can know what the psalmist expressed when he said, "Cast your cares on the Lord and he will sustain you; he will never let the righteous fall" (Psalm 55:22).

Remember also the words of my beloved disciple John: "This is the confidence we have in approaching God: that if we ask anything according to his will, he hears us" (1 John 5:14). When I hear, I answer. Let that assurance fill you with peace.

In prayer as in all of life, you can put your trust wholly in me in full assurance that I am fulfilling my purpose. Whether the problem or trial is yours or another's, be assured it will not last too long. The briars on the path will do no permanent damage to those who have chosen to walk with me. My followers will be blessed, protected, strengthened, and provided for.

As you hand your prayer concerns over to me, I will lighten your load. I am your burden-bearer. My words recorded by Matthew are applicable to you:

> Come to me, all you who are weary and
> burdened, and I will give you rest. Take

my yoke upon you and learn from me, for I am gentle and humble in heart, and you will find rest for your souls (Matthew 11:28,29).

❧ 22 ❧

Feelings of Stagnation

ord, *you have brought me a long way. You have indeed kept all your promises. I join the psalmist in saying, "Great is your love toward me; you have delivered me from the depths of the grave" (Psalm 86:13).*

You comforted my heart and healed
the hurts which had me in their grip.
And I thank you.

But now I seem to be growing so
slowly. It seems I progressed more
rapidly while I was going through all
that pain than I am now. I feel as if
I'm at a standstill, making no
progress at all. Shouldn't I be further
along my path than I am? What's
wrong with me?

*D*ear child of mine, there's nothing wrong with you. Your will is to do my will. You're beginning every day with me—in my Word and in prayer and meditation. That's my desire for you. You have simply fallen back into that old habit of being too hard on yourself. I am "a compassionate and gracious God, slow to anger, abounding in love and faithfulness" (Psalm 86:15). So leave yourself alone.

Remember, growth is a never-ending process. No one ever *arrives* in this life. Besides, it is *I* who do the work in you. Recall the words of Paul: "He who began a good work in you will carry it on to completion until the day of Christ Jesus" (Philippians 1:6). Have you not considered that I sometimes put my children in a "waiting place" for reasons known only to me? I accomplish my work in you in ways you don't understand.

I am always at work in my yielded children. Don't expect too much of yourself. Neither give up your dreams. Recapture your visions. Reclaim the territory which the enemy of your soul has sought to take from you.

Keep in mind: "'I know the plans I have for you,' declares the Lord, 'plans to prosper you and not to harm you, plans to give you hope and a future'" (Jeremiah 29:11). Just as you trusted me in the past to work in you, trust me now. I have not changed. Neither have my promises. Keep your eye on my promises.

When you feel as if you're not going forward in your walk with me, the enemy uses that feeling to discourage you. He would like for you to doubt that you hear my voice. Do not believe him when he appears with that trick. "[I call my] own sheep by name and lead them out. . . . [my] sheep follow [me] because they know [my] voice" (John 10:3,4). Listen and you will hear.

I call you to joy.

I call you to victory.

Expect great things of me and of yourself because I live within you.

Surrender your all to me.

Lean on me.

Wait on me.

Depend on me.

Although you may not realize it, I have glorified my name through you because of your faithfulness during your trials of the past. I will glorify my name through you again. Your part is to be sensitive to my voice. Be sensitive and quick to obey. You will be blessed and you will be a blessing.

> Trust in the Lord with all your heart and lean not on your own understanding; in all your ways acknowledge him, and he will make your paths straight (Proverbs 3:5,6).

❧ 23 ❧

Optimism Lacking

ord, you know I wasn't born an optimist. Some people seem to always feel good about life and everything that happens. I usually have to work on my emotions, reminding myself often that you're in

charge and that I can trust you to
work things out for my good. What
can I do about this characteristic
which I don't like about myself?

*B*eloved child, you are as I created you to be.
Accept yourself as you are. If you were naturally optimistic, you would feel self-sufficient and
fail to keep in touch with me. My desire above all else
is intimacy with you. You were created for fellowship with me.

You *are* learning how to tune out negative thoughts.
You can congratulate yourself on that. To experience
occasional defeat doesn't mean you're a failure. Everyone loses battles now and then. But you never lose the
war as long as you're holding my hand.

Don't be embarrassed to talk to yourself when
you need to boost your optimism. David did it all the
time. Listen to these words of his:

> Why are you downcast, O my soul? Why
> so disturbed within me? Put your hope in
> God, for I will yet praise him, my Savior
> and my God. My soul is downcast within
> me; therefore I will remember you (Psalm
> 42:5,6).

In the midst of his dismal feelings, David often

made such declarations as this: "No one whose hope is in you will ever be put to shame" (Psalm 25:3).

Making such affirmations helps to move your intellectual concepts from your mind to your heart. That's where you're lacking. Intellectually, you know the truth about my faithfulness and that you can afford to be completely optimistic at all times, but your heart hasn't grasped the message.

Continue as you're doing and you will see a gradual change in yourself. You are already changing; you just don't see it. Remember that any process is slow. Keep listening to tapes based on my truth. Keep reading inspiring books that encourage and uplift you.

Avoid listening too much to negative news events. Your sensitive mind holds them in your consciousness and you become too absorbed in what is going on in the world. Focus on my power to bring about change. I am at work in all things. That includes you, my dear one.

·24·

Waiting

ord, you know I've always been an impatient person. I dislike waiting. Regardless of what it is, I want it now. I realize this is unhealthy both spiritually and emotionally. But why do you so often require us to wait when you know how difficult it is? I suppose impatience is a form of not trusting you. But what can I do about it?

*D*ear child of mine, waiting is a necessary part of walking by faith. If you never had to wait for an answer, or if you received every desire instantly, you would be self-sufficient. You wouldn't need me. I created you to be dependent upon me. I want your fellowship.

Waiting causes you to lean on me, to look to me for support. Waiting stretches your faith. Waiting requires you to give up control of a portion of your life. You're relinquishing that part of yourself to my control.

What can you do to be more patient? First, keep your eyes on me. Remember, it is your desire for *me*, not your desire for *things*, that's most important in your life. I will supply, but material things are secondary.

Focus on the present, not the future. Live now. *Now* is my gift to you. Enjoy it. Concentrate on what you can do for yourself and others today.

If your desire is of me, it will be fulfilled in my timing. Your life and your circumstances are in my hand. You cannot see me at work, but I am always working in your behalf. Realize that my requiring you to wait for me to act is part of my discipline for you.

Waiting in anxiety will drain you of strength. Have you noticed when you wait anxiously how the enemy tempts you to doubt my faithfulness? Next you start to worry about the outcome of your hopes. After that the enemy accuses you of anything you allow him to.

Waiting in trust will energize you. Waiting can help you to look at things from my perspective. Your security is in me, not in the outcome of your dreams. "So do not throw away your confidence; it will be richly rewarded. You need to persevere so that when you have done the will of God, you will receive what he has promised" (Hebrews 10:35,36).

·25·

Disturbed

*ord, I know your Word says
we are to have no anxiety
about anything. I believe that includes
living without being disturbed about
what goes on in our world. But I find
I can't watch the evening news*

without becoming quite disturbed. The reporters give us the ugly details of everything. Hearing their voices and seeing the accompanying scenes makes it as real as if it were happening in my living room.

I always view what I see and hear as a call to prayer. But then I forget that you are more real than happenings and I find myself becoming disturbed and overly burdened.

*S*ensitive child, indeed I do want you to live without disturbedness. "A calm and undisturbed mind and heart are the life and health of the body" (Proverbs 14:30 AMP). Remember that regardless of what goes on around you, I hold you in the hollow of my hand.

I understand how easy it is for my concerned children to become obsessed with the problems of today. But if you're not careful, you'll drown in unnecessary anxiety about problems over which you have no control.

Continue to pray and intercede for those involved in and affected by the news, then release your burden to me. I care about the situation more than you, and I am able to deal with it without your dwelling on it. My desire is that you live so rooted and grounded in me and my love that you allow nothing to shake you. I am more real than anything that goes on in your world.

As never before, you must live in an intimate relationship with me and rely on me for wisdom, knowledge, and protection. This is a time for every child of mine to "be self-controlled and alert. Your enemy the devil prowls around like a roaring lion looking for someone to devour" (1 Peter 5:8). He knows his time is short and he is marshaling his demons to attack wherever he can.

Remember the words of my servant Peter: "Casting the whole of your care [all your anxieties, all your worries, all your concerns, once and for all] on Him, for He cares for you affectionately and cares about you watchfully" (1 Peter 5:7 AMP).

Remember also the words of the psalmist David:

> Cast your cares on the Lord and he will sustain you; he will never let the righteous fall. But you, O God, will bring down the wicked into the pit of corruption. ...But as for me, I trust in you (Psalm 55:22,23).

❧ 26 ❧

Weariness

*Lord, I don't mean to complain,
but I'm tired, tired of having to
be the strong one, tired of never
getting everything done that needs
doing. The calendar says my body is a
few decades old. I feel it. But on the*

inside I'm still a little girl, a little girl
in need of her Father's comfort and
strength.
    Help me to draw upon your
strength, to feel your strong arms
holding me up.

*M*y **little girl**, I know how tired you are. I see that your reservoir of strength is temporarily low. Fortunately for you, mine never is.

    My strength is perfect
    When your strength is gone.
    Come to me and rest awhile.
    Breathe deeply of my energizing flow of
       life.
    As you believe, so shall your strength be.
The government and care of your life
    are not for your shoulders
    but for mine.
Let my peace which transcends all understand-
    ing guard your heart and mind and give you
    rest.
The world has tried to squeeze you into its mold.
The voice of the world says,
    Accomplish more,
    work faster,
    rise up early,

stay up late,
perform,
get ahead.
All of this is vain.
Set goals and work from them,
  but work from a position of rest,
  not from anxiety.
Your life must have
  balance,
  relaxation,
  recreation.
Listen not to the world.
  Heed your own inner voice.
  Be true to the spirit I've put within you.
The world offers imitations of success.
  Its way is the path of
    struggle,
    pressure.
I offer you abundant life,
  a life of
    rest,
    joy,
    peace.
You will come through your time of weariness,
  not only strengthened
    but encouraged,
  knowing that I have strengthened you
    with power through my Spirit.
You will rejoice in me.

You will know it was I who made you strong,
　who blessed you with might.
Never doubt it, child of my heart:
You are indeed strong in me.
　Those who hope in the Lord
　will renew their strength.
　They will soar on wings like eagles;
　they will run and not grow weary,
　they will walk and not be faint
　　　(Isaiah 40:31).

❧ 27 ❧

Problems with
Meditation

ord, *even though I've known you as Savior and Lord ever since I was a young girl and am blessed with many excellent Christian books and teaching tapes and have gone to numerous spiritual retreats, I still sometimes have difficulty stilling myself and tuning out distractions during my quiet time. This concerns me.*

Beloved child, I understand your concern. The rush and activity of a busy life indeed scream for your attention when you sit down to be alone with me. I'm glad you realize that you must learn to still your own thoughts and emotions in order to sense the flow of my thoughts.

You are acquainted with Psalm 46:10—"Be still, and know that I am God." To be still is to relax and let go. Have you discovered that *struggling* to still yourself only makes you tense? The more you *pressure* yourself to tune out unwanted thoughts, the more agitated you become.

As you seek to calm yourself, pay attention to the quiet of the early morning. Hear the sound of birds singing, joining you in your praise to me. Be aware of my presence all around you. Realize my greatness. Present your whole self and your feelings to me.

Use your breathing to bring yourself to a greater awareness of my presence. As you exhale, breathe out all doubt and negativity. As you inhale, breathe in my love.

If in the midst of your meditation you suddenly remember an urgent task that you're fearful of forgetting, write it down. (Keep a pen and paper handy for that purpose.) Then dismiss the thought. As for other interruptive thoughts, ignore them and they will pass. Don't fret or scold yourself. Just bring your thoughts back into focus and proceed with your meditation.

Never allow the enemy of your soul to discourage you regarding your time with me. Some mornings if you feel that you're accomplishing nothing, return to reading my Word. Let the Scripture suggest a thought. Then close your eyes and meditate on it. Think about how that particular Scripture passage may apply to your present situation.

Being still is focusing on me, realizing that I am your very breath. Practice my suggestions and you will find that stilling yourself becomes easier as time goes by. Remember not to try to force anything. Simply enjoy my presence. On those days when you feel nothing, know that I am present. You don't have to feel my presence in order to know that I am with you.

Go your way now and know that you're being made whole.

PART TWO

❧

He Answers
My Friends

❧ 28 ❧

Shannon's Grief

ord, I find no relief for my pain. I thought my husband's lengthy illness prepared me for his homegoing. But a curtain has been drawn, never to be reopened. I'm like a child alone in a dense forest.

Sometimes I feel as if I'm waiting
for something to happen, but what?
Will my night of sorrow never end?

*P***recious child**, I feel your hurt with you. Though it seems long, your night of sorrow *will* end. Morning will come.

Meanwhile, allow yourself to grieve. Grief is a process to work through. It is a healthy reaction to the shock and emotional aftermath of death. When you feel like crying, don't try to control your tears. Tears are healing.

Sometime after C.S. Lewis said goodbye to his wife for the last time, he said grief is like a long winding valley where any bend may reveal a new landscape. You, dear child, will eventually discover that new landscape. God "heals the brokenhearted and binds up their wounds" (Psalm 147:3).

Be assured you're not alone. I am with you. When you feel the stab of intense pain, pour out your feelings to me. Talk to me about your departed one. When darkness settles over you with renewed blackness, remember that your dear husband is safe and happy with me.

Meditate on such passages of my Word as these:

My help comes from the Lord, the Maker
of heaven and earth. He will not let your

foot slip—he who watches over you will not slumber; indeed, he who watches over Israel will neither slumber nor sleep. The Lord watches over you—the Lord is your shade at your right hand. . . . The Lord will keep you from all harm—he will watch over your life; the Lord will watch over your coming and going both now and forevermore (Psalm 121:2-5,7,8).

May I gently remind you that it is in the valley of trial that I give strength. It is in the blackness of night that my light shines most brightly. It is in the seeming emptiness of life that my blessings flow most abundantly. I will become more real to you than ever before. "Never will I leave you; never will I forsake you" (Hebrews 13:5).

❧ 29 ❧

Dena's Hopelessness

Lord, I feel caught in a sea of desperation with no way out. Everything presses me down. Remember, I live alone except for my teenage drug-abusing son. I am threatened with job loss. What will become of me?

*O*verly *concerned child of mine*, you've allowed yourself to become bogged down in the mire of hopelessness. Please realize I haven't forgotten you.

I am your ultimate source of help. "Call upon me in the day of trouble; I will deliver you, and you will honor me" (Psalm 50:15). That was my reminder to the psalmist. It's also my reminder to you. If you lose your job, it will be for the best. You will find another in my time.

I will provide for you. The psalmist David declared:

> I was young and now I am old, yet I have never seen the righteous forsaken or their children begging bread. . . . For the Lord loves the just and will not forsake his faithful ones (Psalm 37:25,28).

That includes you.

As I was with the three Hebrew children in the fiery furnace, so I am with you. As those Hebrew boys came to a place of complete confidence in me, so can you. You will learn to trust me and wait. You will not be disappointed. I never forsake my own, though it may seem for a season that I have. Each of my children must learn in his or her own way to trust me and me alone.

Most of my children go through times when they feel I am far away. But I have planted hope in your heart. You can bring that hope to the surface by praising me, although I know you don't feel like it. David discovered praise to be a wonderful antidote for despair. He learned to praise me at all times, even in the depths of despair:

> I will extol the Lord at all times; his praise will always be on my lips. . . . I will praise you as long as I live. . . . I will praise you, O Lord, with all my heart; before the "gods" I will sing your praise (Psalm 34:1; 63:4; 138:1).

I invite you to praise me in spite of your circumstances. Praising is not denying a situation. It is recognizing that I am sovereign. I will intervene. I have unlimited resources.

‹ 30 ›

Laura's Expulsion

Lord, I've been ostracized from my Christian group. I attended an interdenominational retreat where I saw the truth that faith in Christ frees us from the works of law. My church fellowship teaches that you

*accept us on the basis of perfor-
mance. My friends haven't seen you
as a loving Father. They serve you out
of fear, not out of love and devotion.*

*Thinking my friends would be as
happy as I to know the good news of
freedom in Christ, I shared it with
them. I made the mistake of reading
to them J.B. Phillips' translation of
Galatians 3:3—*

> *Surely you can't be so idiotic as
> to think that a man begins his
> spiritual life in the Spirit and
> then completes it by reverting to
> outward observances.*

*I'm hurt and disappointed. What
shall I do?*

*H*urting child, I understand your feelings. I
too was rejected by my friends. I know how it
hurts.

How sad that so many of my children feel more
comfortable with a set of rules than with letting me

live my life through them. I long for them to know
that I am a personal God who enjoys closeness with
them.

I rejoice that you have found the joy of my indwelling presence. Since your group has shut you out
and refuses the liberating truth you have found, why
not look for another fellowship? I will lead you to one
where you can receive more truth.

You will continue to grow in your understanding
that you are precious in my sight simply because you
are mine. You will enjoy companionship with those
who have learned that mature Christianity is not a
matter of theologizing *about* me, but of *knowing* me
and accepting and walking in the knowledge of my
love.

You will experience greater and greater joy in
knowing that everything you do while walking in the
Spirit is motivated by me. All of your service will be
motivated, not by oughts and shoulds as in the past,
but by your love for me. You will become increasingly aware of the meaning of Paul's words:

> I have been crucified with Christ and I no
> longer live, but Christ lives in me. The
> life I live in the body, I live by faith in the
> Son of God, who loved me and gave him-
> self for me (Galatians 2:20).

❧ 31 ❧

Vera's Divorce Anguish

ord, I'm devastated. After thinking all these years I had a storybook marriage, I suddenly find myself divorced. Unprepared for the shock when my husband announced he planned to marry one of my best friends, I sat speechless. It's hard to believe my Christian husband and my good friend could do this. How can I bear the pain when I feel so rejected and alone?

*B*eloved child, I feel your pain. I see your tears and I will comfort you. I have not forgotten you.

> Can a mother forget
> > the baby at her breast
> > and have no compassion
> > on the child she has borne?
> Though she may forget,
> > I will not forget you! (Isaiah 49:15).

Do not be afraid
> to draw near to me,
> to develop an intimate relationship with me,
> to trust me completely.

You may tend to compare me with those who hurt you. I understand. I do not condemn you.

My love is
> clean,
> pure,
> holy,
> undefiled,
> has no self-gain in mind.

I will always be a faithful lover to you.

Arise, my darling,
   my beautiful one,
   and come with me
   (Song of Solomon 2:10).

I realize my words may sound unreal to you.
They're contrary to all you have experienced. Listen
with spiritual ears while I tell you:

The Lord your God is with you, he is
mighty to save. He will take great delight
in you, he will quiet you with his love, he
will rejoice over you with singing (Zephaniah 3:17).

Spend time alone with me regularly. Share with
me every secret, every fear, every hope, every dream.
I'm never too busy to listen.

In our times together you will discover depths of
truth you've never seen before, meaningful promises to lean upon.

Do not be afraid; you will not suffer shame.
Do not fear disgrace; you will not be hu-
miliated. You will forget the shame of
your youth and remember no more the
reproach of your widowhood. For your
Maker is your husband—the Lord Almighty is his name—the Holy One of
Israel is your Redeemer (Isaiah 54:4,5).

Many times you've heard, "In all things God works for the good of those who love him, who have been called according to his purpose" (Romans 8:28). You may feel like asking, "But what about this situation, Lord?" Yet in your heart you know I cannot lie.

Meditate on this promise from the Amplified Bible:

> I will not in any way fail you nor give you up nor leave you without support. [I will] not, [I will] not, [I will] not in any degree leave you helpless nor forsake nor let [you] down (Hebrews 13:5).

Be assured of my continual, comforting presence. "Arise, come, my darling; my beautiful one, come with me" (Song of Solomon 2:13).

❧ 32 ❧

Jane's Desperation

Lord, I've been praying and waiting for months for another job. As a single mother I feel desperate. I wonder daily about how I am going to provide for my children. What can I do?

*B*eloved child, be assured I have not forgotten you. Although your situation looks desperate to you, I am in charge. You're going through a testing time because of the nation's economy and because of the fallen world in which my children live.

But I would not have allowed you to arrive at this place of desperation if I had not intended to help you. You and your children will never go hungry.

I live in you to help you. I, in all my power, wisdom, and goodness, am on your side. You are part of my family. You can know the truth the psalmist declared. It applies to you.

> God is our refuge and strength, an ever-present help in trouble. Therefore we will not fear, though the earth give way and the mountains fall into the heart of the sea, though its waters roar and foam and the mountains quake with their surging (Psalm 46:1-3).

You need not be swept into the undertow of stressful times. I am for you. I "will meet all your needs according to [my] glorious riches in Christ Jesus" (Philippians 4:19). You can depend upon me and upon my resources. I never let my children down.

True, your last job ran out. But my resources never do. Because you are my child, I have assumed responsibility for you. You are not a victim of the economy. I am quietly at work in your behalf. Wait and you will see what I am about to do.

Let this time of waiting be an occasion for deeper relationship with me. Ask for my wisdom in dealing with your circumstances. Listen to my quiet voice. I will guide you in the right path to an open door. Do not allow the enemy to discourage you if the answer is slow in coming. I am never late.

·33·

Erma's Depression

ord, I feel depressed. The daily load of stress is too much for me. I feel chronically tired, anxious, worthless, and helpless. I know I'm your child, so I'm sure I shouldn't feel this way. I ought to be

*in control of myself and my
emotions. So I feel guilty. Are you
rejecting me? What can I do?*

Beloved child, please be assured that I'm not
rejecting you. I never reject my children. Let
go of your guilt. Depression is not a sin. The intensity
of a person's emotional suffering is often in direct
proportion to his intensity of devotion to me.

All Christians experience what one of my recent
servants called three levels: *Mountaintop days*, when
everything looks rosy; *ordinary days*, when they're
neither elated nor depressed; *dark days*, when they
feel their world is tumbling in on them. Obviously
you're now experiencing *dark days*.

Saints in both the Old and New Testaments went
through periods of depression. Look at the book of
Psalms. Remember, David was a man after my own
heart. Consider the many times he called out to me
in a state of depression. On one occasion he cried:

> How long, O Lord? Will you forget me
> forever? How long will you hide your
> face from me? How long must I wrestle
> with my thoughts and every day have
> sorrow in my heart? (Psalm 13:1,2).

But David refused to remain long in a state of
depression. Immediately after crying out in desperation, he declared:

But I trust in your unfailing love; my
heart rejoices in your salvation. I will
sing to the Lord, for he has been good to
me (Psalm 13:5,6).

David knew that I loved him and would come to
his rescue. He sang to me even when he didn't feel
like singing. I love you, dear one, no less than I loved
David. I invite you to soak your soul in the Psalms.
Linger with passages that speak to your heart.

Take refuge in me. I will spread my blanket of
protection over you. In the day of Moses, I instructed
him to appoint cities of refuge for the pursued. There
they found safety and protection. I am an even more
certain refuge for you.

Come and take refuge in the shelter of my wings,
where there is warmth and protection, love and provision. "Taste and see that the Lord is good; blessed
is the [one] who takes refuge in [me]" (Psalm 34:8).

No one who takes refuge in me will be disappointed. Whether it is a person or a circumstance
from which you need protection, I will rescue you.
My unfailing love for you reaches far beyond the
assaults of the enemy. You can trust yourself to my
care. As an eagle shelters her little ones with her
wings, so I will protect you with my strong arm.

He who dwells in the shelter of the Most
High will rest in the shadow of the Almighty. . . . "Because he loves me," says the

Lord, "I will rescue him; I will protect him, for he acknowledges my name. He will call upon me, and I will answer him; I will be with him in trouble, I will deliver him and honor him" (Psalm 91:1,14,15).

That means you, precious child. You can rest in the knowledge of my love and sufficiency. In those times when you don't feel like reading your Bible or praying, simply sit quietly or lie down and meditate on Scripture or on my love for you. You need not struggle to give me anything. Simply open yourself to receive from me. You are mine. I love and accept you.

❧ 34 ❧

Gina's Doubts

Lord, *if you are the God of love and power that I'm told you are, why do you allow all these problems in my life? As soon as one problem is solved, another arises. Surely you're a long way from me.*

eloved, **misguided child,** problems must come but they are never of my making. I'm never far from you. You sound like my Old Testament friend Gideon. When I sent my angel and told him I was with him, "Gideon replied, 'If the Lord is with us, why has all this happened to us? Where are all his wonders that our fathers told us about . . . ?'" (Judges 6:13).

Many others also have asked this question. David often briefly doubted my presence when problems loomed large before him. On one occasion he cried, "Awake, O Lord! Why do you sleep? Rouse yourself! Do not reject us forever. Why do you hide your face and forget our misery and oppression?" (Psalm 44:23,24). So you see you're not alone in your doubts and frustration.

Have you been deceived by the books that promise easy success to the Christian? Such books leave out the reality of battles and struggles, and promise only victory. I never promised a life free of difficulty. How would you grow if you never faced anything you couldn't handle without my help?

But remember, I am never the cause of problems. Problems come because of the fallen world in which you live. That was true with Gideon and David, and it's true with you. Some problems come from people who don't know or love me. Others come from circumstances over which you have no control. Some result from your own misdirected decisions.

I'm sorry to say that some of my children allow their disappointment to drive a wedge of resentment between me and them. Be careful that you don't yield to such temptation. Problems have the power to make you either better or bitter.

Problems are a part of life. I am aware of your weakness and inadequacy to solve them on your own. You can trust me to help you solve every problem. You will discover there's no problem too big for me. The only problems that can defeat you are those you try to handle without me.

I am always a strength for my people, a fortress of salvation for my chosen. You are strong in me and in the power of my might. Remember, when a problem looms before you, I am present with you. I am your strength. You have only to look to me. Focus on me and my love. Trust me.

‎35‎

Ina's Guilt Feelings

Lord, my feelings of guilt weigh me down. No matter what I do, I feel guilty, even though my rational mind tells me I'm innocent. I know you've forgiven me, but I can't shake this feeling of guilt. What's wrong with me?

*B*eloved child, you're like many others for whom the truth of forgiveness has never moved from intellectual understanding to assurance in the heart. I'll tell you why.

In childhood you were given rigid standards and impossible goals by your well-meaning parents and teachers. Self-blame and inferiority feelings resulted. Now as an adult, you are continuing the pattern of expecting the impossible of yourself. You are focusing on your weaknesses and human frailties. Then you're subconsciously punishing yourself by feeling guilty.

Unwarranted guilt feelings are rooted in a distorted view of me. I am a God of love. I do not demand instant maturity of my children. Only *I* can bring you to maturity. Turn your eyes from yourself to me.

You have never had a full revelation of the depth of my personal love for you. You feel you need to analyze your every motive and action. Dear child, you're taking your own spiritual temperature. Leave that to me. I want you to learn to relax in my love and be yourself. Know that I accept you just as you are. I'm not condemning you.

If you sin, I'll send conviction into your heart to let you know. Shall I tell you how to distinguish between conviction from me and self-condemnation? Condemnation is nagging and general, implying that you're worthless in every area. Conviction is specific. I convict only to help you, to show you an area of your life in which I want to work.

My voice is always gentle and uplifting. The enemy's voice is urgent and often depressing. He condemns in order to destroy. I convict in order to restore and set free.

In your daily quiet time focus on my love, not necessarily praying, but feeling my loving presence. Learn to accept yourself because I accept you in Christ. I live within you to make you what I created you to be. "Therefore, there is now no condemnation for those who are in Christ Jesus" (Romans 8:1).

❧ 36 ❧

Christy's Despair

ord, I don't know what to do. I seem to get nowhere when I try to pray. Nothing improves or changes. I'm lacking in faith, so maybe you don't hear me.

I feel like crying with Job, "If only

I knew where to find him; if only I could go to his dwelling! I would state my case before him and fill my mouth with arguments. I would find out what he would answer me, and consider what he would say" (Job 23:3-5).

My prayer differs from Job's only in that I don't know how to "state my case" or what to argue. I only know that I'm miserable and unworthy and don't know what to do about it.

*P*recious child, if only you knew how much I love you, your tower of misery would quickly collapse. I bought you with the precious blood of my Son. You are of great value to me.

As for your lack of faith, consider the words I inspired my apostle Paul to write: "If we are faithless, he will remain faithful, for he cannot disown himself" (2 Timothy 2:13). My faithfulness to you depends not on your faith but upon my everlasting faithfuness.

The enemy of your soul has deceived you. He planted thoughts in your heart and you believed that those thoughts came from me. He made you feel far away from me, unworthy to call upon me. You are worthy through Jesus, the Son of my love. I love you as I love Him.

I sent my beloved Son to justify all who trust in me. He was a perfect representation of me, my exact likeness, a perfect demonstration of my love.

Consider how much my Son loved His disciples. I love you no less. You are forgiven. You are redeemed. Your past is

> blotted out,
> paid for,
> forgotten,
> cast into the sea.

You have received grace and mercy. I never revoke my gifts. My righteousness does not allow for nullifying anything I have given. I change not (Malachi 3:6). Enter into the joy of knowing who you are in me. Declare who you are:

> free from condemnation (Romans 8:1);
> free from the law of sin and death (Romans 8:2);
> my redeemed child (Luke 1:68);
> one of my chosen (1 Peter 2:4);
> accepted in the Beloved (Ephesians 1:6 KJV);
> made righteous through Christ (2 Corinthians 5:21);
> blessed with every spiritual blessing (Ephesians 1:3);
> complete in Christ (Colossians 2:10 KJV);
> hidden with Christ in me (Colossians 3:3);
> always led in triumph (2 Corinthians 2:14).

Because you are in me, you may approach me with complete freedom and confidence. Come boldly before my throne of grace. Rest in the assurance of my unconditional love.

Be assured that my invitation is always open for you to come to me with your burdens, your cares, your frustrations. I will never turn you away, because through my Son you are made worthy.

❧ 37 ❧

Sara's Codependency

ord, I'm worn out from trying to please everyone. I've been told my problem is codependency. I thought a codependent person was an alcoholic, a drug addict, or a person who lived with one. I've never been in either of those situations. So how could I be codependent?

ear child, a codependent person is anyone who seeks the approval of another person to fill the void that only I can fill. But the label is not important. Let's simply look at your needs and find the best way to meet them. You admit that you're worn out from trying to please everyone. Have you considered *why* you must please others? May I tell you? You are obsessed with the need to be needed and appreciated.

You are my child. You are as valuable as the people whose needs you're trying to meet. Dear one, why must you meet others' needs at the expense of neglecting yourself and your own needs? Your spiritual enemy has deceived you. He has told you that your self-worth comes from the approval of others, and you believed him.

Dear child, it is I who gives you worth. You're trying to get others to fill an inner void no human being can fill. You have been going through life trying to make others happy in return for the evasive feeling of being loved. You need never look to others to give you the assurance that you're worthy and lovable. I, your Creator, declare that you are already everything that you want others to tell you you are.

Just as my beloved Son, Jesus, knew I loved Him, I want you to know I love you. As I said to Him, "You are my beloved Son," so I say to you, "You are my beloved child." As He lay down each night, not mentally going over His day to decide whether He had pleased everyone in his path that day, but only His Father, so I want you to do.

You please me by being yourself, not by doing for others at the expense of your own physical and emotional health. Live in tune with me and let me direct you to those who need your help. Let your service for others be motivated by your love for me, not by whether others will be pleased with you.

You need time to *be*, not simply time to *do*. "Be still, and know that I am God" (Psalm 46:10). Not in the busyness of doing for others and hoping for their affirmation, but in the stillness of your heart, *listen* while I affirm you.

Practice an awareness of my presence. In that awareness each day, get in touch with your deep feelings, and together let's deal with them. Recognize that past circumstances resulted in your coming to false conclusions about yourself and your needs. Of course you cannot change anything that happened in your past, but with my help you can change your response to those happenings.

My will is that you stop taking unnecessary responsibility for the lives of others. Practice tough love, requiring others to do for themselves what they're capable of doing. Let them learn to depend on *me*, not on you.

If you continue to be overburdened, join a caring group of believers. My healing grace flows through my loving, caring children. I am he "who comforts [others] in all [their] troubles, so that [they] can comfort those in any trouble with the comfort [they themselves] have received from God" (2 Corinthians 1:4).

Remember that overcoming any longstanding problem is a process. I am a patient Father. So be patient yourself, "being confident of this, that he who began a good work in you will carry it on to completion until the day of Christ Jesus" (Philippians 1:6). Never forget that you are my beloved child.

·38·

Betty's Loss
of Purpose

Lord, the recent happenings in my life have left me with nothing to live for. I feel little but inner pain. I no longer have any purpose in life. I feel like crying with the psalmist, "Out of the depths I cry

to you, O Lord; O Lord, hear my voice.
Let your ears be attentive to my cry
for mercy" (Psalm 130:1,2).

*D***ear child of mine,** I understand your cry and the reason for it. I realize you have given up your hopes and dreams. But I will heal your hurt. You can recapture your visions and your former expectations.

You can reclaim the territory the enemy has sought to take from you.

Trust me.

Trust my Word.

Trust my promises.

Do not listen to the voice of the enemy. He has told you that your life now counts for nothing. Do not believe him.

I call you to joy.

I call you to victory.

Expect great things of me and of yourself.

I will redeem your past. I will use the things that have happened, that have almost crushed you. Nothing will be wasted.

Lean on me.

Wait on me.

Depend on me.

I will glorify my name in you and through you.

I will be exalted as you look to me in hope and confidence.

You cannot see the way ahead, but I can. I have set you apart for myself for my particular purpose. You will be blessed and you will receive a blessing. Hold fast to that assurance.

My strength is perfected in your weakness. Do not try to see ahead. As the manna was fresh every morning, so my strength is new each new day. As your day, so shall your strength be.

Declare with the Old Testament prophet: "The Sovereign Lord is my strength; he makes my feet like the feet of a deer, he enables me to go on the heights" (Habakkuk 3:19).

❧ 39 ❧

Sally's Pain
of Loss

Lord, I can't put into words the depth of sorrow I feel. So much of my joy has gone since the passing of my loved one. I didn't know it would hurt so badly or last so long.

The shock of her homegoing numbs

*me. I cannot understand why she had
to go. I am not blaming you, for I
know your Son came to give life, not
to take it. But that understanding
doesn't make my pain any easier to
bear.*

*P*recious hurting child, I know the pain you
feel. I am aware of your feelings of heaviness,
of despair and anguish. I know and I care. "As a
mother comforts her child, so will I comfort you"
(Isaiah 66:13).

Sometimes you would like to fly away from life
and from this situation which you feel is almost too
much to bear. I understand.

I know you long to be with her, but you realize
you must continue your journey here. Be assured
that I don't ask you to stop the tears. Let them flow as
long as you need to.

It's all right for you to keep asking, "Why did this
have to happen?" But never forget that I am with
you. I will never leave you. When you are tempted to
ask if I care, join the hymnwriter in answering with
all sincerity:

O yes, He cares, I know He cares,
His heart is touched with my grief;
When the days are weary,

> The long nights dreary,
> I know my Savior cares.*

Put your trust wholly in me. Your valley of sorrow will not last too long. Only those who seek their own selfish ways come to lasting sorrow. You have chosen to walk with me. You will be blessed, protected, and strengthened.

One day you will join your loved one and know the truth of John's words: "He will wipe every tear from their eyes. There will be no more death or mourning or crying or pain" (Revelation 21:4). On that day you will be among those who shout:

> Hallelujah! Salvation and glory and power belong to our God. . . . Hallelujah! For our Lord God Almighty reigns. Let us rejoice and be glad and give him glory! For the wedding of the Lamb has come, and his bride has made herself ready (Revelation 19:1,6,7).

---

* Frank E. Graeff, "Does Jesus Care?" (copyright Hall-Mack Co., 1901).

∾ 40 ∾

Gwen's Timidity

Lord, my problem may seem small to everybody else, but it makes me miserable. I often feel paralyzed by shyness. I dislike being shy and it makes me dislike myself. Is anyone else as shy as I am? Why am

I shy? Must I always live with the scourge of shyness?

ear timid child of mine, you're not alone. There are many other miserably shy people— people so shy that their dreams are shattered and their careers threatened. You're not as shy as they.

No, you are not doomed to a lifetime of shyness. And precious one, be assured you don't have to visit a psychologist to change your pattern of behavior.

The reasons for shyness vary. Shyness sometimes indicates a lack of self-acceptance. One of *your* problems is that you expect too much of yourself because your parents were overly strict. But don't blame them. No one has perfect parents.

With my help, you can take responsibility for your life and overcome much of your shyness. When you see that you fall short of your standards, you feel you're a failure. That drives you to crawl into your hole of shyness. It's okay to be weak. "My grace is sufficient for you, for my power is made perfect in weakness" (2 Corinthians 12:9).

Loosen up, dear child. "A cheerful heart is good medicine" (Proverbs 17:22). Learn to laugh at yourself and your mistakes. The world won't fall apart when you make a mistake.

Recognize the fact that shyness has some good points. Since you are sensitive about your own feelings, you are thoughtful of how others feel. You are careful not to offend. Shy people are often more creative than others because they usually spend more time alone than most.

It may make you feel better to know that many people experience shyness at times. They often hide it, so you may not know it when your friends have times of shyness.

You can change the way you feel about yourself, dear child of mine. Remember, all growth is slow, so don't expect to change overnight. I will send people into your life to help you overcome your shyness. Watch for opportunities when you can express yourself comfortably. Do it without fear.

I made you a unique individual. Develop a strong sense of your identity by being more aware of my love and grace. Accept yourself, knowing I love you just as you are.

❧ 41 ❧

Tera Questions God's Love

Lord, I'm struggling with the feeling of your personal love for me. I can accept your universal love for the world, but how can I know you love me as an individual when I'm so weak and undeserving?

The night I accepted your salvation,
the minister read John 3:16, and I
knew it included me, but now I have
doubts. I don't feel your love.

*D*oubting **child of my heart**, you're like many of my growing children. You expect to continue to feel that exhilaration you felt when you first experienced my love. You accepted me as Savior instantaneously. But you must grow in understanding the depth my love. Discovering the vastness of my love is a lifelong process.

Most of my children are slow to grasp my unconditional love. You tend to think you have to earn my love because you equate me with your human parents. You had to live up to certain standards in order to please them. That was a part of your disciplinary training. Your parents' love was conditional, just as is all human love. But I love you simply because I *am* love. It is my nature to love.

I, who made you in my image, love you infinitely. You are my precious redeemed child. Of course you are weak. So are all my children. I love you no less than if all your efforts succeeded. My heart of compassion always reaches out to you. I want you to rest in my love. Allow my love to sink deeply into your heart.

Your value is not based on anything you accomplish but upon who I am. The world measures your value by your achievements. I never do. Nothing can quench the fire of my love for you.

As soon as you awaken every morning, say to yourself, "God loves me. I am His very own child. I am valuable to Him. He accepts me just as I am. He chose me. He adopted me. Nothing can separate me from His love." Meditate on those thoughts.

You may feel foolish at first. Never mind. Meditating on those words every morning will fix them in your mind. Something within you may want to deny what you say. Ignore that voice. You are agreeing with my Word.

Every night before you fall asleep read Paul's prayer for the Ephesians, but personalize it as follows:

"I pray that out of his glorious riches he may strengthen me with power through his Spirit in my inner being, so that Christ may dwell in my heart through faith. And I pray that I, being rooted and established in love, may have power, together with all the saints, to grasp how wide and long and high and deep is the love of Christ, and to know this love that surpasses knowledge—that I may be filled to the measure of all the fullness of God" (Ephesians 3:16-19).

Read the prayer slowly and meditatively, closing your eyes at intervals to realize that this is my sincere desire for you. Yes, dear one, I really love you.

❧ 42 ❧

Ella's Self-Flagellation

ord, *I'm aware that I'm much too hard on myself. I try to accomplish more in a day than is humanly possible. But I don't know how to change my behavior pattern.*

Precious child, I'm glad you have come to me with your problem. Your low self-image is keeping you from developing into the beautiful, happy person I created you to be. You have told yourself that you don't deserve to be joyful and relaxed. You think you have to keep busy accomplishing things for me and for others, and that to be still and enjoy beauty is a waste of time.

You realize that you are not taking time to do the recreational things you enjoy doing. Your life is out of balance. You're failing to do the very things that will nourish your soul and spirit. Would you treat your best friend the way you're treating yourself? Would you deprive your child of the things she needs? Is it I who pushes you to strive as you're doing? No. "The Lord is good to all; he has compassion on all he has made" (Psalm 145:9). I want you to learn to see yourself as I see you and treat yourself as I treat you.

Let the things you do come from the deep awareness of my love for you, not because you feel driven to work for me. Rest in my love before doing anything else. Remember Jesus' words to His twelve apostles: "As the Father has sent me, I am sending you" (John 20:21). Notice that He said, "*As* the Father sent me. . . ." How did I send Him? First of all, I sent Him out in the full knowledge of my love for Him.

My Son felt utterly secure in me because He knew how much I loved Him. You, like too many of my children, have gone out to work in my kingdom without first fully grasping my abiding love. You have intellectual knowledge of my love, but you lack the heart understanding which you need.

You are putting yourself down because you feel as if you're not doing enough. I would be satisfied if you would *do* less and *be* more. Be more alone with me. Enjoy me and the beauty I've created for your enjoyment and mine.

Solomon was right when he said, "However many years a man may live, let him enjoy them all" (Ecclesiastes 11:8). Enjoy life, knowing that I am with you, living in you and working through you to fulfill my purpose.

❧ 43 ❧

Lea's Problem
with Hearing God

*ord, I hear a lot of talk about
how to hear you speak. Some
of my friends say they receive your
guidance through visions. Others say
you speak only through your written
Word. I'm confused. What shall I*

*believe? I want to be sure that I
follow your voice alone.*

ear child, first saturate yourself in my written Word. Drink deeply at my fountain of
life. "All Scripture is God-breathed and is useful for
teaching, rebuking, correcting and training in righteousness" (2 Timothy 3:16). Listen to my Spirit
speak through my written Word, and you will not go
astray.

I'm continually speaking through my written
Word for those who are willing to hear. When you
read my Word, and suddenly a certain passage seems
to leap to life, that is my particular Word for you at
the moment. My Spirit, who inspired the writing of
my Word, speaks to you when you read it. He brings
personal meaning to certain words which are applicable to you.

Some people misunderstand this concept. They
play the "name-it-and-claim-it" game. Taking a passage out of context, they say, "That's something I
want. I'll claim that promise as mine." Then they try
to manipulate me and circumstances until they receive their desire. That is not my way.

Of course, I desire the best of everything for all
my children. But as a good Father, I give what is best
at the time that's best for each individual. I may
need to teach them some things before they are
ready to receive.

I occasionally speak through visions, but be assured I never give guidance that doesn't agree with my Word. I and my Word are one. I never contradict myself, and I never change my mind.

Sadly, some of my children have been led astray by visions. A vision or voice which cannot be verified by my written Word is not of me. It is either the person's imagination or the enemy. Your spiritual enemy is a counterfeit. Have nothing to do with those who claim to have had a vision which cannot be substantiated by Scripture.

"My sheep listen to my voice; I know them, and they follow me" (John 10:27). You can be sure my voice is always gentle and kind, firm and decisive, never harsh or demanding. When you hear a word of prophecy from men, test their words by my Word. Men's words must agree with my written Word.

44

Beth's Childhood Trauma

Lord, I'm still hurting from what my uncle did to me when I was a child. Even though it happened many years ago, the memory of the ugly event still sometimes haunts me, and I feel the same terror I felt then.

In spite of my present beautiful home life, I sometimes feel as if I'm living in a lonely prison of shame and disgust. I've never told anyone but my husband. He is sympathetic but he cannot understand the pain I feel. Must I live the rest of my life with these ugly feelings?

Precious innocent child, I see your unshed tears and feel your lingering hurt. I will heal your memory and ease your hurt.

No one else, not even your husband, can understand how you feel. However, you might feel better if you would confide also in your closest friend. You probably would be surprised at how sympathetic she would be. And she could lend prayer support, especially on those days when you're feeling particularly miserable.

You can find some release by writing your feelings in a confidential notebook. Record the feelings that surface during your daily prayer and Bible reading time. Look for and meditate on Scriptures that especially speak comfort to your heart.

My Son surely included you when He spoke these words:

The Spirit of the Lord is on me, because

he has anointed me to preach good news
to the poor. He has sent me to proclaim
freedom for the prisoners ... to release
the oppressed, to proclaim the year of the
Lord's favor (Luke 4:18,19).

The good news He brings to you, my poor mis-
treated child, is that I know and care and will set you
free. I sent my Son to proclaim freedom from your
prison of shame and to release you from the painful
memories of your past.

The cry I issued to Isaiah is still—

"Comfort, comfort my people," says your
God. . . . He tends his flock like a shepherd: He gathers the lambs in his arms
and carries them close to his heart (Isaiah
40:1,11).

I long to comfort you, to hold you close to my
heart as a gentle shepherd of the East cared for the
lambs of his flock.

I have chosen you and have not rejected
you.
So do not fear, for I am with you;
do not be dismayed, for I am your God.
I will strengthen you and help you;
I will uphold you with my righteous right
hand. . . .

For I am the Lord, your God,
who takes hold of your right hand
and says to you,
"Do not fear;
I will help you" (Isaiah 41:9,10,13).

On the cross my Son felt the pain you feel. It was for you that He bore the pain.

He was despised and rejected by men, a man of sorrows, and familiar with suffering. . . . Surely he took up [your] infirmities and carried [your] sorrows . . . and by his wounds [you] are healed (Isaiah 53:3-5).

Although your painful memory lingers in your deep mind, it can be healed, not by striving, but by realizing ever increasingly how much I love you. My love is a healing ointment to which nothing can compare. Meditate often on my love for you. When others fail you, I remain faithful. My love never diminishes.

I have begun a good work in you. I will continue. I will replace your ugly memories with my beautiful promises. When you feel painfully vulnerable, remember that I cover you with my robe of righteous love. You are mine, beloved child of my heart.

◦ 45 ◦

Toni's Problem of Knowing God's Will

ord, I'm hearing a lot of talk about how to know your will. I'm not sure if I know how to determine your will. All this talk frightens me. I don't want to make a wrong decision. How can I know your will?

Child of my heart, I want to remind you first of all to relax in my love. You have committed your life to me. I am in charge. Would I allow one to go astray who is walking humbly before me, reading my Word daily, talking to me, and sincerely desiring to follow me in every detail of life?

"He guides the humble in what is right and teaches them his way. All the ways of the Lord are loving and faithful for those who keep the demands of his covenant" (Psalm 25:9,10).

You are living under the new covenant. My wisdom and guidance are not written in a lifeless blueprint. I do not guide you with an outside list of rules and regulations. I speak to you from within, through a Person, my Son. Instead of giving you a list of directions, I have given you Jesus, the living Word.

I plant my will in the desires of your heart. If you're concerned about making a certain decision, you can be safe in praying, "Lord, if it is your will for me to do this, increase my desire to do it." If your desire decreases, don't do it. If it increases, go ahead in full assurance that I'm leading you. I'm assuming, of course, when you pray that prayer, that you have chosen to do my will.

When you study the journeys of my apostle Paul, you see a good example of one who knew that my will was built within his own desires. On one occasion after Paul and Barnabas had spent some time in Antioch, Paul said to Barnabas, "Let us go back and visit the brothers in all the towns where we preached the word of the Lord and see how they are doing" (Acts 15:36).

You will notice Paul didn't say, "Let's pray about going." Paul knew if I didn't want him to go, I would somehow turn on a red light and stop him. However, if you ever run a spiritual red light, you can still know that I am able to work things out.

As you grow in your knowledge of me, you will grow increasingly sure of my direction. Relax and enjoy the journey. Trust your own inner voice, knowing that I live within you and that I am your life. Join Paul in declaring, "For to me, to live is Christ" (Philippians 1:21).

❧ 46 ❧

Sherry's Misery over Her Abortion

Lord, I know you've forgiven me for the abortion I had when I was young, but I still feel miserable when I think about it. I still hear the doctor's words ringing in my ears, affirming my suspicions—

*pregnancy, and then his assurance
that I needn't worry. "An abortion is a
simple procedure of removing some
tissue," he declared.*

*Oh, if I had only thought for
myself instead of listening to a man
who probably didn't know you and
who had no respect for the sanctity
of human life. If I had had the
courage to talk to a Christian friend,
I could have spared myself this
lingering misery. I know I can't undo
my sin. What can I do, Lord, besides
thank you again for forgiving me?
How can I alleviate the pain I feel?*

*B*eloved hurting child, you know you were
deceived by the enemy. You know also that
I've forgiven you. But you're allowing the enemy to
keep you in bondage to your past. You must let your
past go. Rejoice in knowing that one day you will
have the joy of holding your precious innocent one in
heaven.

Meditate on the good news of my cleansing blood.
Realize that all your sins are washed as white as
snow. You have an intellectual knowledge of that

fact, but your heart needs a greater revelation of my love and forgiveness.

Each time you take communion, take a moment to dwell on the significance of my shed blood. Remember that wonderful clean feeling that engulfed you the day you accepted my salvation. I want to restore the joy of your salvation.

When accusations come, meditate on these words:

> The blood of Jesus, his Son, purifies us from all sin.... If we confess our sins, he is faithful and just and will forgive us our sins and purify us from all unrighteousness (1 John 1:7,9).

Come to me often. Let me comfort your heart. Dwell on such words as these:

> [He] forgives all [my] sins and heals all [my] diseases, [he] redeems [my] life from the pit and crowns [me] with love and compassion.... The Lord is compassionate and gracious, slow to anger, abounding in love.... For as high as the heavens are above the earth, so great is his love for those who fear him (Psalm 103:3,4,8,11).

I never waste anything. Because of your past, I will make you a blessing to others. Rejoice and be glad.

~ 47 ~

Peggy's Loss
of a Loved One

Lord, you alone know the pain in my heart. I've never known such intense emotional anguish. Coming home from the hospital without my precious one is almost too much for me to bear. The cloud

*engulfing my soul is heavier than the
ominous clouds in the sky this
morning. Why did my dear one have
to die so young?*

*I cry with the psalmist, "In the
morning, O Lord, you hear my voice;
in the morning I lay my requests
before you and wait in expectation"
(Psalm 5:3). I turn daily to your Word
for strength, but I find so little help.
Is it normal for me to feel as I do?
The pain in my heart is so great. How
can I handle it?*

*P*recious grieving child, I hear your cry. I feel
your pain. The things you're feeling are normal. Every grieving person experiences what you're
feeling at this time. Acceptance of your loss and healing of your hurt will come, though perhaps slowly. I
want to bear your heartache and comfort your heart.

Early death comes partly because of the fallen
world where your spiritual enemy exercises so much
control. "The thief comes only to steal and kill and
destroy; I have come that they may have life, and
have it to the full" (John 10:10). Though your life
seems without purpose at this time, remember that

I am the foundation on which you will rebuild your life.

"The last enemy to be destroyed is death" (1 Corinthians 15:26). Until I come again, you suffer the sting of death. But one day death will be swallowed up in victory (1 Corinthians 15:54). Taking time often to review such truths can give you strength and encouragement.

You are familiar with the following Scriptures. You may find comfort by lingering with them:

> Even though I walk through the valley of the shadow of death, I will fear no evil, for you are with me; your rod and your staff, they comfort me (Psalm 23:4).

> The Lord gives strength to his people; the Lord blesses his people with peace (Psalm 29:11).

> The Lord's unfailing love surrounds the man who trusts in him (Psalm 32:10).

> I am the resurrection and the life. He who believes in me will live, even though he dies (John 11:25).

> Do not let your hearts be troubled. Trust in God; trust also in me (John 14:1).

> In my Father's house are many rooms; if it were not so, I would have told you. I am

going there to prepare a place for you. And if I go and prepare a place for you, I will come back and take you to be with me, that you also may be where I am (John 14:2,3).

The day will come when you will experience the truth expressed by John:

He will wipe every tear from their eyes. There will be no more death or mourning or crying or pain, for the old order of things has passed away (Revelation 21:4).

Until then, lean heavily upon me, knowing that I care.

·48·

Renee's Fears

ord, *I feel so fearful most of the time. I feel utterly helpless to do anything about my situation. The Bible speaks of the fear of the Lord. Is it right for me to be afraid of you? I'm afraid of a lot of other things too. Is there anything I can do about my fears?*

ear child, when you read in Scripture about the "fear of God," it does not mean being afraid of me. You have noticed that Solomon said, "The fear of the Lord is the beginning of wisdom" (Proverbs 9:10). He meant that it is wise to honor me, acknowledge my greatness, and recognize my exalted position. Remember that when you read in my Word to fear me, it means you are to respect and reverence me.

To fear me is to trust me. Trust in me is meant to remove all fears. The psalmist said, "I sought the Lord, and he answered me; he delivered me from all my fears" (Psalm 34:4).

A reasonable sense of fear is healthy. Fear of danger keeps your young child from running out into the street in the path of an oncoming car. It may keep you from throwing caution to the winds regarding diet, exercise, and the health of your body.

But spiritually you need not fear, since you know me as Savior. Remember the words of Paul to young Timothy:

> God did not give us a spirit of timidity,
> but a spirit of power, of love and of self-
> discipline (2 Timothy 1:7).

Your spiritual enemy would like to paralyze you with fear to keep you from being of service to me. He knows if he can fill you with fear about your personal adequacy, you will do little or nothing to further my kingdom.

When that kind of fear comes, remember that I don't ask you to be successful—only to be obedient and to know that it is I who am working through you.

Learn to trust me with all your desires—whatever you want to be and do. Trust me to meet all your needs, regardless of their nature—spiritual, physical, or material.

> Trust in the Lord with all your heart and lean not on your own understanding; in all your ways acknowledge him, and he will make your paths straight (Proverbs 3:5,6).

❧ 49 ❧

Tammy's Concern for a Wayward Son

ord, *for years I've prayed for my son, but it seems my prayers are not heard. I see no change whatever in him. He has no apparent interest in anything having to do with you or the church. He doesn't even want me to talk to him about his relationship with you. What will it take to bring him to you? My burden is heavy.*

*P***recious concerned mother**, I feel the ache in your heart. I hear your prayers. Be assured they will be answered. But as with everyone, I have given your son a free will. I will not violate his will. In due time he will see the light and turn to me. Meanwhile, pray in trust and confidence in me, not in anxiety.

Dear one, one of the first things you must do is release your son to me. Your mother-heart naturally wants to hold on. When you let him go, I will be able to work more freely in his life.

Remember the parable my Son told about the prodigal son? Notice that He made no mention of the father trying to locate his lost son or bring him back home. That father's heart ached just as yours does for your child. When the son came to himself, he returned home.

One day your son will also come to himself. He will realize that I paid the price for his salvation. When my Spirit convicts him and reveals my great love for him, he will be unable to resist any longer. But the conviction must come from me, not from any human being.

Since you brought up your son to know me, you can be assured he will return.

> All your sons will be taught by the Lord, and great will be your children's peace (Isaiah 54:13).

> [You] will not toil in vain or bear children doomed to misfortune; for [you] will be a people blessed by the Lord, [you] and [your] descendants with [you] (Isaiah 65:23).

> This is what the Lord says: "Restrain your voice from weeping and your eyes from tears, for your work will be rewarded," declares the Lord. "They will return from the land of the enemy. So there is hope for your future," declares the Lord. "Your children will return to their own land" (Jeremiah 31:16,17).

Realize that I am as concerned for your child as you are. Meditate on the above Scriptures and be at peace.

❧ 50 ❧

Anna's Questions About Knowing God

Lord, I'm disturbed. I've trusted you for salvation, and I don't doubt that I have eternal life because your Word says, "Now this is eternal life: that they may know you, the only true God, and Jesus Christ, whom you have sent" (John 17:3). In that sense I know you, but I'm sure I don't know you as fully as I should.

I certainly can't claim to know you as well as the apostle Paul. After years of walking with you, he said his determined purpose was to know you and to become more intimately acquainted with you (Philippians 3:10 AMP).

What is this all about? I've evidently missed something. I study your Word, but I have a feeling that knowing you includes more than studying about you. What does it mean to know *you?*

Inquiring child, I'm glad you asked. Indeed you are not to stop at knowing me only as Savior. The kind of knowledge referred to in the verse you quoted indicates a growing experience with me. You must understand the difference between knowing *about* me and knowing me. You know *about* me by studying Scripture. But to know only *about* me is to miss many blessings I want to give you.

When you were in high school studying biology, you analyzed a flower, studying its various parts.

You knew enough about the flower to pass the test without difficulty. But you received no particular blessing from your knowledge.

Last week when you drove past a bed of colorful phlox, you stopped and enjoyed them. Your first thought was of me. You worshiped me and thanked me for creating such beauty. In that moment you celebrated life. You were blessed.

I am not to be analyzed but to be spiritually tasted. "On the last and greatest day of the feast, Jesus stood and said ... 'If anyone is thirsty, let him come to me and drink'" (John 7:37). The psalmist, who knew me as well as any Old Testament writer, said, "Taste and see that the Lord is good" (Psalm 34:8).

Remember that my Son said, "Just as the living Father sent me and I live because of the Father, so the one who feeds on me will live because of me" (John 6:57).

Take time to feed on me. Realize that I am in you, and you will begin to experience what it means to know me in the true sense of the word.

Harvest House Publishers

For the Best in Inspirational Fiction

IN TOUCH WITH GOD
How God Speaks to a Prayerful Heart
by *Marie Shropshire*

Knowing how to have life-giving fellowship with God in the midst of life's challenges is the key to fulfillment in the Christian walk. From this personal journal we learn that there is no difficulty or wound that is out of reach of His healing touch.

HIS IMPRINT, MY EXPRESSION:
Changed Forever by the Master's Touch
by *Kay Arthur*

Times of joy refresh us; times of loneliness and confusion break down our walls of self-sufficiency. Our experiences become tools in God's hands—gently used to shape and polish our lives. These candid and deeply personal devotions speak with warm honesty about the trials we face and the unconditional love of God that sustains us. Discover with Kay the transforming power of a moment-by-moment relationship with Jesus Christ and the wonder of listening to God's still small voice bring a special beauty to our lives—the unmistakable imprint of the Master.

THINGS HAPPEN WHEN WOMEN CARE
by *Emilie Barnes*

Things Happen When Women Care shows you how to carve out time for others by streamlining the details of daily living and home organization. This warm, insightful look at developing friendships and enlarging the boundaries of your personal ministry will give you the tools you need to start today on the great adventure of caring for others.

QUIET MOMENTS FOR WOMEN
by *June Masters Bacher*

Though written for women, this devotional will benefit the entire family. Mrs. Bacher's down-to-earth, often humorous experiences have a daily message of God's love for you!

THE CONFIDENT WOMAN
by *Anabel Gillham*

Anabel Gillham was trying hard to be the total Christian woman—until she found out that's not what God wanted. Like Anabel, you may have tried hard to make your life work—and believed that if you tried hard enough to be the total Christian woman, God would honor your efforts. The liberating truth is that God does not want you to be a *total* Christian woman, but a *confident* Christian woman—one who is sure how much God loves and accepts her. Walk with Anabel as she shares how you can experience your *own* unshakable identity in Christ and find the strength to meet life's circumstances.

THE BONDAGE BREAKER
by *Neil Anderson*

Jesus intends for us to win the spiritual battles that confront us daily and He has provided everything we need to gain the victory. Yet instead of experiencing victory, we often find ourselves trapped in defeat—overcome with frustration, bitterness, and discouragement. If you have ever found yourself enslaved by negative thought patterns, controlled by irrational feelings, or caught in habitual sinful behavior, Neil Anderson can help you understand the strategy of Satan and fight back.

15 MINUTES ALONE WITH GOD
by *Emilie Barnes*

Speaking as someone who has been there, home-management expert Emilie Barnes responds to the cries of women who can't find time for consistent devotions and Bible reading. While helping to develop consistent study habits, Emilie shares from the Bible and her heart meditations of encouragement and direction. The devotions, especially written for busy women, include thoughts on prayer, hospitality, grace, and other subjects close to the heart and home.

Dear Reader:

We would appreciate hearing from you regarding this Harvest House nonfiction book. It will enable us to continue to give you the best in Christian publishing.

1. What most influenced you to purchase *God Whispers in the Night*?
   ☐ Author   ☐ Recommendations
   ☐ Subject matter   ☐ Cover/Title
   ☐ Backcover copy   ☐ _____

2. Where did you purchase this book?
   ☐ Christian bookstore   ☐ Grocery store
   ☐ General bookstore   ☐ Other
   ☐ Department store

3. Your overall rating of this book:
   ☐ Excellent   ☐ Very good   ☐ Good   ☐ Fair   ☐ Poor

4. How likely would you be to purchase other books by this author?
   ☐ Very likely   ☐ Not very likely
   ☐ Somewhat likely   ☐ Not at all

5. What types of books most interest you?
   (check all that apply)
   ☐ Women's Books   ☐ Fiction
   ☐ Marriage Books   ☐ Biographies
   ☐ Current Issues   ☐ Children's Books
   ☐ Christian Living   ☐ Youth Books
   ☐ Bible Studies   ☐ Other _____

6. Please check the box next to your age group.
   ☐ Under 18   ☐ 25-34   ☐ 45-54
   ☐ 18-24   ☐ 35-44   ☐ 55 and over

Mail to: Editorial Director
Harvest House Publishers
1075 Arrowsmith
Eugene, OR 97402

Name _____

Address _____

City _____   State _____   Zip _____

**Thank you for helping us to help you
in future publications!**